P R

WHEN FAITH DISAPPOINTS

"Lisa Fields compassionately confronts the brokenness and failure of the human condition through the lens of faith, yet brilliantly offers hope for all who seek to practice their faith without the cruel dogma nurtured by Western culture. A worthy addition to your personal library."

—OTIS MOSS III, senior pastor of Trinity United Church of Christ, Chicago

"Wisdom and empathy fuel Lisa Fields's new book, *When Faith Disappoints.* Drawing from her wealth of experience as an apologist and her story as a doubter, Fields offers a work that centers and normalizes our doubts and fears. She doesn't give pat answers but rather both wisdom and the power of presence, while approaching with care some of the most compelling questions of our day."

—DR. CHRISTINA EDMONDSON, co-author of *Truth's Table*

"Lisa Fields has accomplished the rare feat of writing a book that would be useful for people inside and outside the faith. Christians who have struggled with doubt and disappointment, and those considering the claims of

Christianity, will find themselves challenged and inspired. Her book is not the mere apologetics of the mind; it is more than that. It contains the hard-won wisdom of someone who has done her own wrestling with God and, for that reason, has mercy upon those who doubt. I highly recommend it."

—ESAU MCCAULLEY, PHD, author of
How Far to the Promised Land

"*When Faith Disappoints* is a timely and transformative guide for those navigating the complexities of faith deconstruction and reconstruction. Drawing insightful parallels from the struggles of biblical figures such as Jeremiah and Jesus, Lisa Fields reminds us that questioning God is not only permissible but also a vital part of our spiritual journey. She unearths and addresses seven common pain points within Christianity—personhood, peace, provision, pleasure, purpose, protection, and power—and offers guidance and wisdom on how to find solace and meaning amid the uncertainties of faith. This book is a must-read for anyone seeking clarity and who is wrestling with doubt and emotional fulfillment in their spiritual journey."

—LATASHA MORRISON, *New York Times*
bestselling author of *Be the Bridge*

"Few leaders have made Christian apologetics as accessible to common people as Lisa Fields. In *When Faith Disappoints,* she carefully invites those struggling with their faith to question, reconsider, and heal and see God more clearly. This is the perfect book if you, a loved one, or a friend have been disappointed by faith."

—JUSTIN E. GIBONEY, AND Campaign president

"In *When Faith Disappoints,* Lisa Fields gives us permission to wrestle with our questions about God and faith. Her raw, transparent, and vulnerable storytelling is disarming and her hope-filled perspective compelling. A much-needed book for our times."

—CHRISTINE CAINE, founder of A21 and Propel Women

"In a world where faith is often tested by the weight of unanswered questions, *When Faith Disappoints* offers a beacon of hope. Through personal experiences and deep theological reflections, Lisa Fields reminds us that questioning our faith isn't the end but instead the beginning of a journey toward deeper understanding in Christ."

—MARK BATTERSON, *New York Times* bestselling author and pastor

"Lisa Fields's compelling and compassionate book, *When Faith Disappoints,* offers fresh and convicting insight on questions that we all struggle with, while at the same time challenges the reader to pay closer attention to how others are hurting. With transparency and tenderness, Fields gives voice to her own experiences of disappointment and doubt in a way that lets the reader feel seen and understood, and then she gifts us with something better than the easy answers that we want to hear—she hands us tangible hope that we need in order to heal. Reading this book is like receiving a deep-tissue massage: Fields finds the knots and applies truth to specific pain points in a way that leaves you really feeling it. But it is a good kind of ache, and one day soon, you'll move more freely because of it."

—DR. JO VITALE, speaker and co-executive director of Kardia

"Lisa Fields's powerful debut book confronts the realities of suffering and injustice, while firmly rooting her narrative in the faith that heals and empowers. A healing and transformative read that will inspire and encourage you through adversity."

—JON GORDON, bestselling author of *The One Truth*

WHEN FAITH DISAPPOINTS

WHEN FAITH

DISAPPOINTS

THE GAP BETWEEN WHAT WE BELIEVE
AND WHAT WE EXPERIENCE

LISA VICTORIA FIELDS

FOREWORD BY DAVID KINNAMAN

MULTNOMAH

Details in some anecdotes and stories have been changed to protect the identities of the persons involved.

A Multnomah Trade Paperback Original

Published in the United States by Multnomah, an imprint of Random House, a division of Penguin Random House LLC.

MULTNOMAH is a registered trademark and the M colophon is a trademark of Penguin Random House LLC.

Library of Congress Cataloging-in-Publication Data
Names: Fields, Lisa Victoria, author.
Title: When faith disappoints: the gap between what we believe and what we experience / Lisa Victoria Fields.
Description: Colorado Springs: Multnomah, [2024] | Includes bibliographical references.
Identifiers: LCCN 2024000528 | ISBN 9780593601181 (trade paperback) | ISBN 9780593601198 (ebook)
Subjects: LCSH: Faith—Religious aspects—Christianity. | Christian life.
Classification: LCC BV4637 .F43 2024 | DDC 248.4—dc23/eng/20240216
LC record available at https://lccn.loc.gov/2024000528

Printed in the United States of America on acid-free paper

waterbrookmultnomah.com

2 4 6 8 9 7 5 3 1

Book design by Jo Anne Metsch

To my parents, Louis and Lisa L. Fields:
Your example, prayers, guidance, and love have
helped make me the woman I am today.
I love and appreciate you both.
I pray I make you proud.

To my granddaddy Louis Fields, Sr.:
I'm so thankful that you were such a good man.
I miss you and I love you. I am who I am today
partly because of the man you were. I was so
blessed to have you as a granddaddy.

FOREWORD

Being human comes with disappointment built in. We simply can't avoid it. We might even say that experiencing disappointment, disillusionment, and discouragement is simply a nasty case of being normal. Still, these negative experiences often create a weather system all their own, and those downpours frequently wash away people's faith. There's a new name for this storm: deconstruction.

Perhaps you're wrestling with your faith—or you know someone who is and you want to help. Either way, you should know that you're not alone. If you're one of those struggling with disappointment, it really is okay to feel this way.

If you're walking alongside someone who is faltering under the weight of their questions, be patient. And pray! Doubt truly is a normal part of life.

I have the numbers to prove this. I lead a research company that explores the common themes of human experience. We study people's spiritual journeys. Our social research shows that half of adults (49 percent) say they have gone through a period when they significantly doubted their faith. Forty-seven percent agree that "My experiences have led me to deconstruct or take apart the faith of my youth." Sadly, 43 percent assert that "I am disillusioned by my experiences in Christian churches."

What's more, Millennials and Gen Z (people roughly age forty and under) are even more likely to express these sentiments. In their hurt, pain, and disappointment, younger generations' belief in God often swirls down the drain.

When I say you are not alone, I'm referring not just to the numbers.

I have walked my own painful journey of disappointment and disillusionment since Jill, my high school sweetheart and wife of twenty-five years, passed away from brain cancer. Those forty months of disease and death—and all that has followed—have taken me to the deepest places of my faith and my doubts. I've wrestled with God. I've shouted into the heavens to a God who seemed silent. I've groaned and wept and poured out my soul in the aching chasm of loss.

Yet I've learned that Jesus is there through it all. We have a God who comforts us in our heartache and hardship. We follow a Master who bears our pain with us. And God is never scared of our questions and never wastes our suffering. The Christian Scriptures attest to this, and I found my heart pounding at the way the Bible gave voice to—and didn't shy away from—my soul's insurmountable grief and extreme disappointment.

When my friend Lisa Fields asked me to write this foreword, I felt both overwhelmed and honored. Overwhelmed because talking about doubt and disappointment is so difficult and personal. We each have our own private battles, and I want to be helpful and kind—and to point you to Jesus.

I also felt so honored that Lisa asked me to introduce this book to you. I think the world of Lisa, and I am so glad you've picked up her book. In the vast landscape of resources on how to share the gospel, few voices resonate with a profound understanding of the human quest for connection with the divine. Lisa Fields's is such a voice, and in the pages that follow, you'll join her on a journey into the intricacies of faith, doubt, and the relentless pursuit of truth.

Lisa invites us to question, to wrestle, and to explore the space between what we believe and what we experience. In doing so, she unveils a path that leads not away from God but toward a richer, more nuanced understanding of Him.

Lisa is rare in her ability to bridge the gap between the pulpit and the pew. Speaking to both leaders and everyday Christians, she explores the delicate terrain of disappointment with God, drawing from both her own experiences and narratives of the Bible. Her words are simple, cogent, and powerful.

But Lisa doesn't stop at introspection; she also confronts pressing issues of our time. Systemic racism, the marginalization of the Black community—these are not merely topics in her book; they are lived realities she addresses with empathy. In the face of generational racism, Lisa offers a path forward—a call to trust in God as she grapples with the complexities of human history.

One of Lisa's compelling stories centers on the launch of Jude 3 Project. Her vision and mission is to help Black Christians know what they believe and why they believe it. With barely any funds, she faced crushing obstacles. She overcame the harsh realities of bias, racism, and sexism in her pursuit of a mission larger than herself. Early on, she was told, "You're young, a woman, and Black," meaning her chances of succeeding in the white, male-dominated world of Christian apologetics were slim if not impossible.

Yet Lisa did succeed, with the Lord's help, and I am inspired by her leadership!

Reading through the challenges she overcame, from fundraising hurdles to societal biases, from relational pain to struggles of identity, we witness a journey marked by storms. Yet, Lisa reveals every storm has a purpose—a means through which God shapes and refines us. As we navigate the headwinds of our own lives, she reminds us that each trial, every questioning moment, is an opportunity for growth, endurance, and, ultimately, a deeper connection with our Creator.

In these pages, Lisa Fields doesn't just share a story; she invites us into a conversation—a dialogue with doubt, faith, and the God who weaves through it all. It's a conversation that resonates, challenges, and, above all, illuminates the path toward a faith that withstands the powerful storms of doubt.

So, friend, buckle up for a journey that is as inspiring as it is authentic—a journey into the heart of faith, guided by the insightful words of Lisa Fields, a woman of tenacious faith who knows what she believes and why she believes it.

Hers is a rising voice we all benefit from hearing. I am honored to count her as a friend.

DAVID KINNAMAN, CEO of Barna

CONTENTS

WHEN FAITH DISAPPOINTS

PERMISSION TO WRESTLE

Believers should acknowledge and wrestle with
doubts—not only their own but their friends'
and neighbors'.

—TIM KELLER, *The Reason for God*

When I was in seminary, I had a faith crisis. I heard a tragic story about terrorists murdering children in the Middle East. My heart was heavy. I don't struggle as much with why God allows evil to happen to adults, but when children are targeted, I feel differently. They tug at my heartstrings.

I was deeply grieved and began to question God: *Why do You protect some and not others? How can I trust You?*

My mind was spinning, and these thoughts lingered for weeks. I even found it challenging to read my Bible and pray.

Finally, I went to the office of my favorite professor, Dr. Leo Percer, who taught on the New Testament. I appreciated his humility and kindness, so it was a no-brainer that I should seek his guidance.

I explained how I couldn't understand a God who would allow such evil to happen to innocent children. I knew all the arguments for the problem of evil. I could understand that we have free will and that it creates the reality of evil. I could also reason that God uses evil for greater purposes that are sometimes beyond our human understanding. But these logical explanations still left me emotionally unsatisfied. If I couldn't find an answer for why God allowed children to be murdered, then could I continue following Him? Could I keep my faith and trust Him? I paused, holding my breath while I awaited Dr. Percer's response.

He said, "I struggle with that too."

I exhaled. I had expected some deep philosophical or theological answer, but he gave me a very human response. He simply said, "Me too." I thought I was on the verge of losing my faith, but here was a respected professor—with years of knowledge and expertise—who wrestled too. Dr. Percer didn't say anything profound; he was honest about his struggle with God. He normalized my frustration.

Dr. Percer acknowledged that it *is* okay to question God when things happen that I don't understand. After all, my doubts aren't a reflection of my faith in Him. If I could understand everything about God, then I wouldn't need faith. I still question God, and there are still things in the Bible that give me pause and times when I don't understand His ways. The only difference now is that I'm not afraid to ask the hard questions.

Have you ever questioned God? Did you worry that your faith would disappear because you wrestled with His will and His Word? I have good news for you: Wrestling isn't the death of your faith. On the contrary, wrestling is the key to growing in your faith.

> *Wrestling isn't the death of your faith.*

One of my favorite Old Testament scholars, Dr. Jo Vitale, once told me that the way we get to know anyone is through questions and, if that's the case, why would our relationship with God be any different? The first thing we do when we meet someone new is ask them questions. The questions are not to disrespect the person but to get to know them. Similarly, we learn about God by questioning Him. The Bible is full of kings, prophets, and even our Savior wrestling with God.

In frustration, King David asked God,

> How long, LORD? Will you forget me forever?
>   How long will you hide your face from me?
> How long must I wrestle with my thoughts
>   and day after day have sorrow in my heart?
> How long will my enemy triumph over me?[1]

The prophet Jeremiah also had some questions for God:

> Lord, you always give me justice
>   when I bring a case before you.
> So let me bring you this complaint:
> Why are the wicked so prosperous?
>   Why are evil people so happy?[2]

On the cross, even Jesus questioned God: "Jesus called out with a loud voice, *'Eli, Eli, lema sabachthani?'* which means 'My God, my God, why have you abandoned me?'"[3]

You don't have to fear offending Him by verbalizing your questions. He knows your heart and questions, even if you don't voice them. He is your creator. You don't have to be scared. You don't need to run when it gets complicated; you can lean into the questions. God will meet you there.

EMOTIONS AND ANSWERS

In 2014, I founded an apologetics organization called Jude 3 Project that focused on equipping and engaging the Black community. One of my favorite Jude 3 Project events is called Problematic Passages. It's a two-hour

Q and A where the audience gets to question Bible scholars about the verses that trouble them. In addition to this, we had Dr. Esau McCaulley lecture on problematic passages, and he addressed genocide in the Bible. He handled this brilliantly but made a crucial caveat that there is no answer to the question that will be emotionally satisfying.[4] By that, he meant that no answer would make us feel good. And when we get an answer that doesn't make us feel good, we sometimes seek other answers.

As a teenager, I loved football video games. I'd play my favorite, *Madden NFL,* all day. I don't want to brag, but I got pretty good. For me, the highlight of the game was when I scored. As soon as I crossed the goal line, I knew I was closer to winning the game. The goal line is crucial—without it, football would just be people running around endlessly, with no way to determine a winner or the purpose of the game. Likewise, when we ask questions with no goal in sight, we'll never get a satisfactory answer.

I heard one apologist say that before he answers a question about faith, he asks, "If I answer this question to your satisfaction, will you accept Christ?" Why does he do that? He is trying to locate the goal line. He doesn't want to have a purposeless argument about faith; he wants the conversation to head in a particular direction.

Similarly, God doesn't want to argue aimlessly with you. He wants your questions to move you in a specific direction: toward deeper faith and trust in Him. God has a goal line for your questions. What kind of response are you hoping for? What would be a satisfactory answer for you? If you don't know where the goal line is, you'll roam with endless questions that lead nowhere.

MTV has a popular show called *Catfish,* which exposes internet impostors who create fake profiles to deceive people. A person who has formed an online relationship with an impostor wants to believe that the person behind the computer screen is who they claim to be. They've usually been in constant contact with the impostor, receiving consistent, emotionally satisfying stories and answers.

In many cases on the show, when the host presents evidence to the victim that they may have been catfished, the victim denies it. They've been so emotionally satisfied by the lie that they reject the logic of the truth. When they finally accept the facts, they are devastated and hurt. The truth doesn't make them happy; it actually makes them sad. But while the truth isn't emotionally satisfying, it does liberate them from the lies and manipulation.

There can be logical answers to your questions about what God allows and why some people seem protected from things while others don't. The logic won't always soothe your heart; however, an answer doesn't need to be emotionally gratifying to be true. You may still feel pain and confusion, but the truth will always liberate you.

As we dive into the various ways we wrestle with

God—our pain points—and how they influence our view of Him and our faith, remember that our goal line doesn't equate to answers that are emotionally satisfying. The pain and suffering we experience sometimes short-circuit our ability to reason well. Keeping in mind the complexities of how we feel about the truth and the traumas we experience will help us set up a framework as we wrestle with God. Because our goal line is truth and liberation in the gap between what we believe and what we experience.

WHAT IS A PAIN POINT?

A pain point is a complaint. It's an expressed or unexpressed issue a person has with a product, service, or experience. In the business world, CEOs—along with their sales, product development, and customer service teams—devote most of their time and expertise to eliminating any pain points their current or future customers may face. They work diligently, observing every angle of the customer experience. From quality and pricing to product accessibility and delivery, they do everything in their power to ensure their customer has a five-star experience that brings them back for more and prompts them to share their positive experience with others.

One company that has done this exceptionally well is

Amazon. In 2021, their vision was "to be Earth's most customer-centric company, where customers can find and discover anything they might want to buy online, and endeavours to offer its customers the lowest possible prices."[5] Can you hear the pain points they're seeking to avoid? They don't want their customers to be able to complain that they didn't find what they were looking for or that what they found was too expensive. And though not mentioned in their vision statement, their one-to-two-day delivery turnaround shows they want to avoid any complaints about it taking too long for products to arrive. By making it their goal to eliminate every pain point a customer could ever experience through an online delivery service, in 2021 Amazon triumphed over Walmart and became the world's largest retailer outside China.[6]

I often wish God were more like Amazon. I wish He would use His all-knowing, ever-present, and all-powerful qualities to eliminate every kind of difficulty. I want to look at Jude 3 Project—the ministry He has called me to—and tangibly sense that He used His foreknowledge to remove my pain points.

I doubt I'm the only one who feels this way. In fact, I'm certain I'm not. The entire field of apologetics (the theological discipline that helps people give a defense for their faith) exists to address pain points. Though these pain points are presented as philosophical questions, what often lies behind these questions are complaints. For example, behind the question "Why would a good, all-powerful God allow bad things to happen?" is the complaint "God didn't intervene and protect." And there are times when what lies behind questions about sex and sexuality is the complaint "God, Your standards for sexual purity are unreasonably archaic!" or "Why do I have to deny myself something that feels good?" These complaints are pain points.

Over the years, I've come alongside hurting Christians, listened to their pains, and had deep, theological conversations with them. From these talks, I've identified seven common categories of pain points within Christianity, which I'll discuss in individual chapters:

- Personhood (Who am I?)
- Peace (How can I experience a sound mind and tranquility?)
- Provision (How will my needs be met?)
- Pleasure (How can I feel good?)
- Purpose (Why am I here?)
- Protection (How can I be safe?)
- Power (How can I be in control?)

Many have looked to Christianity to answer one or more of these questions. And rightly so. How could we not when the preachers encourage us to find our identity in Christ and we read stories in the Bible about Christ miraculously healing men and women of every kind of disease and feeding more than five thousand people with two fish and five loaves of bread?[7] Is the God of the Bible not full of power? Aren't we to look to Him for peace? Didn't the psalmist say that in His presence is "fullness of joy"?[8] If so, why are Black and Brown people in my country continually oppressed? Why is my parent dying from cancer? Why am I being told to contain my sexuality when it's a big part of how I understand and express myself? The object of our discontent is not a product but a Person whose services aren't measuring up to our expectations or yielding the experience we hoped for.

Pain points exist in the gap between a person's expectations of Christianity and their experience of it—when their faith has disappointed them and they are left wrestling with God. They turned to God because of His promise to give joy, but He doesn't seem to answer, because still daily they are battling depression and isolation. They walked down the aisle to say the prayer of salvation because the pastor told them God wants them to prosper. Then, three to six months later, they find themselves evicted. Out of frustration, they wave their fist at God. Out of hopelessness, they try to discern what they got wrong about Him. They pack their belongings in their car, wondering if the resurrection of Jesus is all a big lie and if God can really make their life better. Does God really keep His word? Is faith in Jesus sufficient for life in a broken world? Does He have any relevance? Does the Cross offer any hope?

To eliminate the pain points, some people have either reframed the Christian faith to suit their needs or left it altogether. Those who have reframed it have created a buffet-style faith. They pick the doctrines and passages in Scripture that they agree with and disregard the rest. Those who have left the faith have stopped trying to reconcile Christianity with their unmet expectations and unanswered prayers, concluding that Christianity doesn't work. Some have even respectfully commented, "Christianity might work for others, but it doesn't work for me." So they've turned to other religious systems and practices to fulfill their need for personhood, peace, provision, pleasure, purpose, protection, and power.

If you find yourself in either of those categories, I want you to know that the goal of this book isn't to criticize or condemn you. Instead, I invite you to reconsider. In the following chapters, we'll explore how the pain points affect us and how rethinking our perceptions of God and Scripture can help us reframe our pain.

Full disclosure: My goal line is also not to *eliminate* the pain points you have with God. As much as I'd like this book to help you completely get rid of your pain points with God, I can't. It would be inaccurate and deceptive of me to make such a declaration since Jesus never promised a life free of pain in exchange for following Him.

Remember, He told His disciples: "In this world you will have trouble."[9] And as someone who believes we live in a fallen world, I've come to accept that I'll wrestle with God in each of these areas until Christ returns and heals all.

As we walk through these pain points, I hope that you'll feel affirmed in your frustration. I hope that the concepts laid out in each chapter will help make your pain or frustration less severe. And I hope that as we address each pain point and engage with the truths of Scripture, you'll no longer feel the need to reframe or reject those truths in an attempt to meet your very valid needs for personhood, peace, provision, pleasure, purpose, protection, and power. I pray that the truth God gave through His Word will result in hope and a resolve to move forward as you cling to a faith that is not only intellectually sound but also growing.

PRAYER

God,

    I don't even know if You're real anymore. I don't know if I made You up and You're just a figment of my imagination. But if You are real, would You prove it to me? I hate to be like Thomas in the Bible, but I need something in order to keep going. I don't want to give up on You, but believing becomes more challenging by the day.

    God, please reveal Yourself to me as I read the pages of this book and wrestle with my doubts and pain.

    In Jesus's name, amen.

PERSONHOOD

My clothes are different, my face is different, my hair is different, but I am somebody! I am Black, Brown, white. I speak a different language. But I must be respected, protected, never rejected. I am God's child!

—REV. JESSE JACKSON, "I Am—Somebody"

While living in Jacksonville, I volunteered with a high school program called the EVAC Movement. The program seeks to empower at-risk youth to escape the cave of despair and hopelessness. One of the students from this program, Glen, received a full tennis scholarship to Florida A&M University, one of the Historically Black Colleges and Universities. At college, he began to wrestle with his faith. Glen reached out to a teacher in the EVAC program for guidance, and she connected him with me.

As Glen and I candidly discussed his struggles, he shared that he was wrestling with whether Christianity was good for Black people or was just a tool of oppression created by white people to harm us. When I asked him what led him to that question, Glen explained, "All the Bible characters are depicted as white, including Jesus, and the Bible has passages on slavery. If Adam and Eve were white, does that mean my skin color is a product of the Fall?"

I paused. Did Glen truly believe his skin color was a product of sin? Did he hate his skin because of that? Did he not see his value as a Black man in the image of God? My heart ached. How many times had I heard that struggle echoed across the globe? How many times had I heard Black people ask, "Are we, too, people made in the image of God?"

Personhood has been a pain point in the Black community for generations. From before setting foot on the shores of America until today, people of African descent have received false narratives about their identity. Not knowing who you are is disorienting, and that pain only intensifies when those who claim to know God treat you like you aren't created in His image.

One of the oldest and most propagated lies from some white Christians was "the curse of Ham"—a lie that sprouted from a story of Noah and his sons. One day, after the Flood, Noah was drunk and naked. His son Ham saw Noah and told his brothers, but his brothers refused to look at their naked father. Instead, they covered Noah. When Noah woke, he found out what Ham had done. Angered, Noah "cursed Canaan, the son of

Ham: 'May Canaan be cursed! May he be the lowest of servants to his relatives.'"[1]

Slaveholders used this passage to argue for Black inferiority. They claimed that God had cursed Ham with dark skin.[2] This misinterpretation of the biblical text led to the narrative that God had cursed all Black people and, therefore, Black people were inferior to the white race. However, a thorough reading of Genesis 9 can quickly clarify this misinterpretation.

First, nowhere in the passage, or when Noah pronounced the curse, was skin color mentioned. Second, Ham wasn't the person Noah cursed; his son Canaan was. Next, God wasn't the one who cursed Canaan. Instead, the curse came from Noah. While the slaveholders' concept of this passage is a clear perversion of the biblical text, the damage to Black self-worth and personhood had a generational effect.

Yet the intentional stripping of Black identity didn't stop with the curse of Ham. The United States' founding fathers added their own tactics for dehumanizing Black enslaved persons. According to the United States Constitution, enslaved people were considered three-fifths of a free person.[3] Fast-forward to today, and we can still see Black people's worth stripped away.

A recent CNN story highlighted how a Black couple's property was appraised at a lesser value because of the color of their skin.[4] When the Black couple initially had their home appraised, the white appraiser valued their house $60,000 under its estimated value. The couple decided to try again but this time staged their house with family photos from their white neighbor. To add to the believability, their white neighbor pretended to be the homeowner when the new appraiser arrived. Consequently, the house was appraised at almost $92,000 more than the initial appraisal.

The disparity in appraisals points to a deeper issue than housing value. Many Americans still don't think Black people have the same value as their white counterparts. They devalue Black people's possessions and their lives. The killing of unarmed Black people in America, such as George Floyd, Breonna Taylor, and Atatiana Jefferson, is a direct contradiction to the Christian ideals that America supposedly upholds.

How can we reconcile a "Christian nation" with one that enslaves Black people and diminishes their humanity? An enslaving Christian nation goes against the very essence of the liberating gospel that we find in the Bible. Jesus said,

> The Spirit of the Lord is upon me,
>   because he has anointed me
>   to proclaim good news to the poor.
> He has sent me to *proclaim liberty to the captives*
>   and recovering of sight to the blind,
>   to *set at liberty those who are oppressed*.[5]

Our Lord came to set us *free,* not to enslave an entire people.

Considering the misuse of the Bible and the current state of this nation, I understand why Glen struggled with whether Christianity was helpful or harmful. He was fed false narratives, manipulated Bible stories, and unjust laws based solely on his skin color. Logically, anyone in his shoes would conclude that they aren't as valuable as others. The history of the United States, its original sin of slavery, and the Christian nationalism some Americans espouse compound the pain and make embracing Christianity difficult for many Black people.

How can something that was used as a tool of oppression be good for humanity? How can the Christian God affirm our personhood when so much harm has been done by the hands and mouths of His supposed children? Does God even care about Black people? When God and His people seem to be the problem, we'll look outside them to find ways to validate our value.

DEIFIED OR DEHUMANIZED

A Black movement and culture called the Five Percent Nation, also known as the Nation of Gods and Earths (NGE/NOGE), popularized the idea that Black people are gods. Their founder, Clarence 13X, believed that "black men are Gods and black women are queens, or

Earths."[6] This ideology entered the mainstream through music artists like Jay-Z and Erykah Badu. Given the history of Black people in America, it has wide appeal. Those who embrace it gain a sense of worth. They move from feeling less than human to divine. However, building an identity around a lie because enslavers gave our ancestors a lie only perpetuates the trauma. The solution to dehumanization isn't deification.

While this ideology may offer a sense of pride and value, it isn't rooted in truth. To be God, you must be infinite, immutable, self-sufficient, omnipotent, omniscient, and omnipresent and possess many other attributes. We can't be God. We were created; God was not. God is in control; we are not. The idea that we could be gods is as old as the Garden of Eden, when Adam and Eve fell prey to the same temptation.

God created Adam and Eve in His own image:

In the image of God he created them;
male and female he created them.[7]

Yet the serpent convinced them to eat the fruit by selling them an identity they already had. The serpent said to the woman, "God knows that when you eat from it your eyes will be opened, and *you will be like God,* knowing good and evil."[8] But Adam and Eve already bore God's image even if they didn't fully understand. When they ate the fruit, Adam and Eve—all of humanity—had to pay an unnecessary price for what they already possessed.

While Adam and Eve's decision may seem obviously wrong, you and I are also guilty. Anytime we pursue worth outside our identity as image bearers of God, we metaphorically eat the fruit. When we aren't secure in who we are and whose we are, we become easy prey and eat a false narrative about our identity. The devil is still whispering in our ears that we can be God. Deification isn't just an issue in the Black community; it's an issue in the white community too.

White supremacy, a pervasive ideology in American history, suggests a "natural superiority of the lighter-skinned, or 'white,' human races over other racial groups."[9] White supremacy has affected every aspect of American society, from our justice system to our churches. It manifests itself in our justice system when white people are given shorter sentences than Black and Brown people. It manifests itself in our economic systems when property values in white neighborhoods are significantly higher than in Black communities. It manifested itself in churches when the Southern Baptist Convention started as a defense of slavery. It manifested itself across America when angry and evil white mobs lynched Black bodies.

White supremacy highlights the evils that ensue when humanity believes the lie that they are more than human. That deception leads to destruction. Evil is a two-way street, and those who enact it don't just damage those they victimize; they also destroy themselves. James said that "each person is tempted when they are dragged away by their own evil desire and enticed. Then, after desire has conceived, it gives birth to sin; and sin, when it is full-grown, gives birth to death."[10] There is no way to do evil without being corrupted by it.

Dehumanization and deification are by-products of deception. Just like Adam and Eve were deceived regarding their identity, we can be easily deceived too. You may feel unsure of who you are, and you may be unaware of your worth, but don't be deceived—you don't need to be God to be valuable. A lie about your personhood will never fulfill you; only the truth about your identity will set you free.

YOU ARE VALUABLE

Every Christmas, my mom puts up two Christmas trees: one in the living room and the other in the den. She decorates the tree in the living room with all modern ornaments, elegant wrap, and lights. By the time she finishes it, it could be photographed for a magazine. But the tree in the den has a different vibe. My mom decorates this tree with all the ornaments my brothers and I designed when we were kids. Most of the ornaments we created as children have either our pictures or our names on them.

While my mom likes the magazine-ready tree in the living room, she loves the tree with her children's ornaments in the den. Even though some of the ornaments have aged, are worn, and have torn, their value in my mom's heart will always remain the same. They aren't valuable to her because they are ornaments; they are valuable because her children's images and creativity are reflected in them.

Similarly, you and I have been given value because, like my brothers' and my ornaments, we carry the image of our creator. When God said in the beginning, "Let us make man in our image,"[11] He meant it. Every man and every woman bears God's image, and that image can't be undone. You are valuable because you are made in the image of God. You will always be valuable because of the image that is on you. Nothing you do and nothing that is done to you will ever take your value.

You are valuable because you are made in the image of God.

God's image is on you, and that's a big deal. However, you will never understand the blessing of His image until you know who He is. God is the creator of heaven and earth and there is no one like Him in all the universe. He is . . .

- infinite (unoriginated)
- immutable (unchanging)
- self-sufficient (need-free)
- omnipotent (all-powerful)

- omniscient (all-knowing)
- omnipresent (always present)
- wise (eternally discerning)
- faithful (unwaveringly true)
- good (perpetually benevolent)
- just (perfectly impartial)
- merciful (endlessly compassionate)
- gracious (forgiving)
- loving (unconditionally)
- holy (transcendent in purity)
- glorious (majestic)[12]

God could have chosen anything else to bear His image—the animals, trees, mountains, or angels. But He didn't. He reserved His likeness for people. The God with all these attributes chose to put His image on you. Doesn't that make you feel special?

Because His attributes are on us, we, like Him, are unique. We are capable of love, goodness, and holiness. While sin may hinder our ability to fully live out some of these attributes on earth, it can never strip His likeness from us. And that image just barely scratches the surface of His deep love for us.

God's love is reflected in His image on us and in the way we were designed. We are "fearfully and wonderfully made."[13] God meticulously designed each feature on our bodies—our heads, our hearts, our smiles, our skin. Every part of us bears the fingerprints of God's design, from our personalities to our noses. God flexed His creativity when He created humans. His attention to detail highlights how valuable we are. And He lovingly calls us His children.

Many parents are unable to articulate the emotions that arise when they see their child for the first time. They feel an intense and indescribable love that they have never known before. A love beyond their comprehension. Their love for their child is not because the child has done anything worthy of love but because the child was made in their image and came from them. Similarly with God: He loved us before we even knew Him, before we put our faith in Him—because when He saw us, He saw His image and knew that we came from Him. It was love at first sight.

Friend, you were cherished by God even before you accepted Him. You may not feel prized by anyone else in your life. You may have been discarded by parents, siblings, or friends, but God loves you deeply. He has enough love to fill the holes left by the people who abandoned you. God's love is relentless. The Bible says, "Nothing can ever separate us from God's love. Neither death nor life, neither angels nor demons, neither our fears for today nor our worries about tomorrow—not even the powers of hell can separate us from God's love. No power in the sky above or in the earth below—indeed, nothing in all creation will ever be able to separate us from the love of God that is revealed in Christ Jesus our Lord."[14]

God loves you so much and thinks you are so valuable that He sent His only begotten Son to die for you.[15] What does it say about your worth that the God of the universe left the comforts of heaven to die for you? Through His actions, God reveals that you are valuable, you are precious, and you are loved. He has gone to great lengths to be reconciled to you. To God, you are worth every sacrifice.

I wish just telling you how much God loves you and how valuable you are would instantly quell all the insecurities in your heart, but I know it's not that easy. Other things still challenge our view of ourselves, and one of them is comparison.

VALUE COMPARED

You've undoubtedly heard it said that comparison is the thief of joy. It's also the thief of our self-perceived value. One of the fascinating accounts in Scripture is the story of Jacob, Leah, and Rachel. Jacob loved Rachel and worked for her father, Laban, for seven years to marry her. When it was time for the wedding, Laban tricked Jacob into marrying her sister, Leah. However, Jacob was so in love with Rachel that even after marrying Leah, he agreed to work for seven more years to marry Rachel. Jacob then had two wives. It should be no surprise that this caused competition between the women.[16]

To make matters worse, Leah was fertile but Rachel was barren. Leah knew that Jacob loved Rachel more, but she also knew she could give him something that Rachel hadn't: children. Every time Leah had a child, Rachel's self-perceived value must have dropped. On the flip side, every time Leah was reminded of Jacob's love for Rachel, her self-perceived value also fell. Their insecurities manifested themselves, and comparison led to competition.

While we may not be sharing a husband with someone else, many of us know what it's like for comparison to affect our self-perceived value. Perhaps your worth takes a hit every time you scroll on social media and find that someone has something you don't. When someone on your timeline gets their dream job and you hate yours. Or when you see an engagement announcement on Instagram and you still can't get a date. Or when you watch a home purchase on TikTok and you are still staying with your parents. Comparison is a reality. All humanity struggles with it. For a long time, I did, too—especially when it came to my career.

I grew up with a plan. I would attend college, major in investment finance, and become a stockbroker. I had picked a job that would give me financial stability. When I graduated, I would be able to get the house and car I wanted. The salary would allow me to travel the world with ease. I had it all planned. However, God surprised me and called me to switch my major to communications and religious studies.

When I graduated, life wasn't how I imagined it. It took me almost a year to find a full-time job. Once I finally found a job, I hated it. At the same time, I had friends who loved their jobs. Each time I compared myself with them, my self-esteem took a hit. From my perspective, my friends were getting all the things I prayed for and God's ears were closed to me. I felt shame around my financial status, and I put unnecessary pressure on myself because of my self-imposed timelines.

When I finally left my job to go to seminary, I entered another season of comparison. I left a paying job to become a broke seminary student while my friends made six figures, climbed the corporate ladder, and took international vacations. Was I not worthy of God's blessings as well? Had He forgotten about me because I wasn't important?

Once I graduated and started Jude 3 Project, I started comparing *again*. I looked at the money we raised versus what other organizations could raise. It seemed so much easier for my colleagues to raise money. However, I noticed that every time I compared, I became more insecure and less grateful. The insecurities blinded me to my value and my blessings.

I wasn't less than because I didn't make as much or because my career didn't seem to be taking off like my friends'. I didn't need to make six figures to be valuable or raise millions to validate my personhood. My worth was not in how much I could make but in who made me. I would be lying if I said I didn't still struggle with comparison from time to time. I still fight to remind myself that my worth isn't in material things.

Can you relate? Are you comparing your life with the lives of your friends, your family, your church members, your co-workers, or those you follow on social media? Are you feeling less valuable because of comparison? Are you struggling with the insecurities that constant comparison brings? I understand. The struggle is real. The apostle Paul addressed comparison when he said, "They measuring themselves by themselves, and comparing themselves among themselves, are not wise."[17] Other people's lives aren't the standard we should base our value on. Don't fall into the trap and allow comparison to overtake you. Remind yourself whose image is on you.

When the Enemy tempted Jesus in the wilderness, Jesus responded to the Enemy's lies with the truth.[18] That is the blueprint for how to handle the temptation of comparison. When comparison tells you that you aren't as valuable as those you see prospering, respond with the truth that you have value because you are made in God's image. Respond with the fact that God sent His Son to die in your place. Respond with how much God loves you. Respond by reciting all the blessings you do have and all the prayers God has already answered for you. You don't have to let comparison win; you can shut down the lies with the truth.

Your value isn't based on what happens in the lives of others. You aren't less human because you don't have all the things you want. You aren't more human because you get everything you prayed for. Nothing outside yourself can affect your personhood. Your humanity and value are based on the design of your creator. Remember this truth when comparison tries to warp your view of your personhood. And remember your value when you inevitably encounter counterfeit identities.

COUNTERFEIT IDENTITIES

"You are more than Jude 3 Project."

My therapist's words sank into my heart. Shock overtook me, and words escaped me. I had been so immersed in my work that, over time, I had made it my identity. I was Jude 3 Project, and it was me. When I saw myself, I saw only my work.

My heart ached and questions filled my head: *How have I connected my identity, my value, to something so tangible, so breakable? What if Jude 3 fails? Who would I be then? How would I know my worth? Who am I without Jude 3 Project?* I needed to find out. I needed to untether my identity from my career, because I was more.

Can you relate? Do you feel the weight of an identity that isn't your own? Have you given a counterfeit identity more value than your true identity? Friend, you are more. You are more than your relationships, more than your gender, more than your race. You are more than your career, more than your bank account, more than your sexual orientation, more than your mistakes and wins. When God wove you together in your mother's womb, He made you His. Just as He is too big to put in a box, so is your identity.

Have you ever tried to put too many groceries in a single bag? When you put a twelve-pack of Pepsi into a plastic bag alongside three apples, two cans of beans, and a bag of chips, what happens? The bag rips, and your groceries hit the pavement. The bag isn't strong enough to carry the weight of the drinks, apples, beans, and chips all at once. Friend, the same happens when you attempt to find security outside your identity as an image bearer of God. The bag of those counterfeit identities will rip and create a big mess of unhealthy relationships, addictions, and trauma.

Any status outside of being a child of God made in His image is a counterfeit identity—and way too small of a view of your personhood. Basing your sense of self on counterfeit identities will always lead to insecurities be-cause these other titles aren't secure enough to hold you. God's image is the only identity secure enough to contain all of us.

Personhood is based on whose image is on you, not what you can achieve or what you do. My therapist re-minded me of that when she told me I'm not what I do. She freed me from the pain of performing. I don't have to compete or pick up counterfeit identities; I can rest in the identity God gave me. I can just exist, being who God made me to be. The same is true of you: You aren't what you achieve.

Your personhood was not earned but given by God. Your negative thoughts and words and your comparison with others can never take away God's gift to you. While the world may try to dehumanize you with their words, images, and laws, they can never strip you of your iden-tity. You were meticulously formed by the divine hands of God, in His image. Therefore, you are cherished, valu-able, and loved. When you understand and embrace His image on you, you will live freer. Walk with your head held high, knowing your identity is secure in God.

PRAYER

God,

I realize that I've placed my identity in things that were too small. When I look in the mirror, I'm often unhappy with who I see—some days, I don't even want to be alive. The taunts from those who have hurt me ring in my ears. If I'm honest, I've come to believe what they say about me more than what You say about me. Their words are ever present, and I say negative things about myself to myself too. I'm trying not to hate myself, but I find it difficult sometimes.

God, help me see myself the way You see me. Please help me see my value. Show me how much I'm loved and treasured by You. Please help me remember when I'm feeling less than that I'm made in Your image.

God, when I'm tempted to put my identity in things that are too small, remind me that being made in Your image is more than enough. I need Your help. I can't do it on my own.

In Jesus's name, amen.

3

PEACE

God cannot give us a happiness and peace apart
from Himself, because it is not there. There is no
such thing.

—C. S. LEWIS, *Mere Christianity*

On a regular Sunday evening in March 2011, my
phone rang and I heard my friend Keisha's familiar
voice on the other end. "Clark got married tonight," she
uttered.

Wait. What? Clark and I had been together almost four
years. I had imagined thousands of times over the years
that Clark and I would get married. I mean, we were
together just last night. Not once had he hinted about a
wedding. I was being punk'd. I had to be. How could the
man I had given my heart to be married to someone else?
*Jump on out, Ashton Kutcher; this has to be one of your famous
practical jokes. Where are the Punk'd cameras?* Nothing
moved.

Keisha kept going, every word piercing deeper and deeper like a dagger. *He chose someone else.* My heart shattered.

Memories of the Valentine's Day card Clark had given me just a month earlier, in which he shared his excitement about our future, filled my head. I had been so full of hope and dreams about our life together. Now the card felt like a cruel joke. A visceral scream surged from within, the long note echoing the profound betrayal I felt.

There's no more Lisa and Clark. Tears blurred my vision. I tried to speak, but my voice betrayed me.

It turned out that Clark, a preacher, had married another preacher. They had been together in the shadows the whole time I knew Clark. Her recent divorce was the escape they needed to go from the darkness to the light. The duplicity was overwhelming. Peace left me that night and was replaced by pain, confusion, bitterness, and anger.

Life has a way of serving us the unexpected—the death of a parent, a cancer diagnosis, the loss of employment—and shaking the foundation of our world. We can't plan for unforeseen circumstances, and even if we could, the pain would nonetheless strip us of our serenity. Sadly, we all experience situations that rob us of our peace. Peace can end up feeling like a rare commodity, and the lack of it takes a toll on our mental health. According to an article from *Forbes,* America is in the middle of a mental health crisis . . .

• 23.1% of U.S. adults experienced a mental health condition in 2022

• As of 2020, suicide is the second leading cause of death for U.S. children ages 10 to 14

• Young adults ages 18 to 25 in the U.S. have the highest rate of experiencing any mental health concerns (33.7%)[1]

While these statistics are startling, they tell only part of the story. The pandemic intensified our nation's preexisting mental health challenges. Grief, fear, economic uncertainty, and heartbreak have been taking a serious toll on our peace these last few years. We are still reeling from the ripple effects of the whole world shutting down.

So we look for relief. Anything to escape from the struggle. But when the pain is palpable, what is the remedy? Jesus said, "Peace I leave with you; my peace I give to you."[2] If He promised to give us peace and we aren't experiencing it, what must we do? How do we move from pain to peace? Do we root ourselves in spiritual disciplines like prayer, fasting, and Bible reading to find peace in distress? And if we do, what happens when those practices that are supposed to bring peace bring none? Do we conclude that faith doesn't work, or are we forced into a new understanding of peace? What actually *is* peace?

THE ROOT OF PEACE

A few months ago, I was teaching a conference workshop with an audience of college students and asked them to define peace.

The students' responses echoed through the room: "Peace is a calm feeling." "Peace is the absence of negative emotions."

I pushed further. "Did Jesus experience negative emotions?"

They paused, thought about it, and responded, "Yes."

I continued. "You're right. Jesus wept when His friend Lazarus died. Jesus experienced so much angst that He sweat drops of blood in the Garden of Gethsemane before His crucifixion. He experienced frustration with His disciples and the Pharisees when they didn't believe, and He experienced heartbreak when He was forsaken on the cross. He experienced a whole range of negative emotions. Yet Jesus was the Prince of Peace, which means He always had peace on this earth. How should that shape how we define peace?"

Friend, the goal of peace is not to escape negative emotions but to not let them control us. Jesus experienced all the feelings we experience but was able to maintain peace because His emotions didn't rule Him. Negative emotions aren't enemies of peace; they reveal whether we possess God's peace.

Paul told the Philippians that God's peace is beyond human understanding.[3] His peace isn't dictated by emotions or circumstances. His peace can't be controlled by fear. God's peace allows us to experience painful events and respond from our knowledge of His character, not from our understanding of our circumstances. Negative emotions are part of the human experience; there is no way to escape them. But we don't have to be led by them.

God's peace is multidimensional and holistic, and it can be divided into three main areas: peace with God, peace with others, and peace within. Peace with God is a gift we have access to through Christ's death, burial, and resurrection. Peace with others is the work of repentance, forgiveness, reconciliation, and restoration in relationships. Inner peace happens when contentment is present, when fear isn't ruling us, and when we confidently face and begin to heal from our traumas. Inner peace is complete trust in God.

To have peace, you need all three areas because they are intricately woven together. You can't have God's peace without having peace with God. You can't have peace with God without having peace with others. And you can't have inner peace if the other two areas aren't present. All aspects of peace are built on one another. The journey to peace is filled with twists and turns, but it can begin only when you have peace with God.

PEACE WITH GOD

When I was in middle school, I had four teeth removed. The dentist gave me a shot of anesthesia before he started to pull my teeth. The anesthesia kicked in within moments, and my mouth went numb. After the dentist ensured I could feel nothing, he began the extraction.

I could hear and see everything happening but couldn't feel anything. He would pause occasionally and ask, "Are you okay?" Then I would nod and he would continue his work. I watched him as he pulled my teeth one by one. When he attempted to remove the last one, the tooth broke. He paused, reached for a different tool, and began digging into my gums. As he searched for the broken piece of tooth, I could see his gloves covered in blood. I began to feel uneasy. *Will he find my tooth before the anesthesia wears off?* I imagined the pain I would be feeling had the anesthesia not numbed me. My stomach turned.

"It's okay," my dentist calmly assured me. I took a deep breath, thankful for the anesthesia. No matter how much he dug into my gums, I felt nothing. But while I didn't feel it at that time, the pain was still present. Anesthesia didn't remove it; the medication just blocked the pain signals from reaching my brain.

We've all used people, places, or things to numb the pain of life. Perhaps you use drugs or alternative spiritual practices to get temporary relief from the angst you experience. Or perhaps you have another route to peace: overeating, television, scrolling aimlessly on social media, sex, travel, shopping, or any number of other practices. If we're honest, most of us use these methods to find temporary relief from pain because we don't want to do the hard work of peace. But they are only numbing mechanisms.

Shortly after I left the dentist's office, the anesthesia wore off and I could feel the pain that had always been present. The numbness was only temporary. Similarly, you can numb yourself with drugs or alcohol, but the pain will be there once you sober up. You can numb yourself with shopping, social media, or food, but after you're done, you'll feel the pain again. Aren't you tired of temporary relief?

Alternative spiritual practices may help you feel peaceful and even give you some tools to cultivate peace in your interpersonal relationships, but they will never give you God's holistic peace, because they can't bring you peace *with* God. You were made to be in a relationship with God, so there will forever be a longing in your soul that can't be satisfied unless you're in a right relationship with Him. A relationship that starts with Jesus Christ.

Before Jesus, God and humanity were at odds because of the sin of Adam. However, Jesus came to create peace between God and us. Jesus forsook the comforts of heaven to put on human flesh. He lived a sinless life but was falsely accused and crucified. His death was the death we deserved because of sin. He took our punishment and received God's wrath on our behalf. He suffered the consequence of our sin so we wouldn't have to. And on the third day, He rose again, making peace possible between God and humanity. When we repent of sin, accept the work Christ has done, and submit our lives to His lordship, God no longer sees our sin; He sees Christ's sacrifice. We are identified not by our sin but instead by Christ's righteousness.

God wants us to experience His holistic peace, but the work isn't only on Him. We are co-laborers in the quest for peace. We must surrender to His process and bend to His will. When we do, we'll experience His presence and a peace unlike any other.

I once heard a pastor tell a story about a flight he was on from Charleston to New York, where the passengers dealt with severe turbulence. Fear gripped his heart, and many people on the plane were visibly scared. However, he noticed that the teenage boy next to him was unmoved. The boy sat calmly, playing his game, utterly unbothered by the turbulence. When the plane finally reached New York, the pastor asked the boy how he could remain so calm on the flight when everyone else feared for their lives. The boy said, "My dad is the pilot, and he doesn't make mistakes." The boy's trust in his father gave him peace in a turbulent situation.

Just like that boy had peace in the chaos because of his trust in his father, you can have peace with your heavenly Father. When you have peace with God, you can bask in the fact that He is with you. You can trust Him because He makes no mistakes.

THE ROAD TO HEALING

A few years ago, I was at a friend's event when Clark walked in. I saw him out of my peripheral. Several years had passed since his wedding. I thought I had moved on. But the mere sight of him disrupted my peace. I was angry all over again. So I avoided him. I told myself I was protecting my peace. I refused to make eye contact and even left the event early. As I was exiting, I saw Clark attempting to get my attention, but I ignored him. I wanted him to know I was still mad.

I had been to therapy; I had thought I was healed. But when I saw Clark that day, I realized I still had more work to do. Therapy was merely the map, not the journey itself. It illuminated the path, but walking the road was on me.

My path led to raw, open conversations with God and community. My friends spoke into the situation that I had been trying to navigate on my own. They guided and challenged me. They helped fill in the gaps of my understanding and prayed with me. While peace filled my heart, it required constant nurturing because the work of peace was never done. It was a path I had to willingly walk each day. At times, the process felt draining, but it gifted me a new life and silenced the revenge in my heart. I was now able to experience life with a healed heart, not a broken one. I could love more freely. Clarity became my portion, and peace became my freedom.

Like me, you may be trying to protect your peace by avoiding situations, people, thoughts, or environments that trigger your trauma. However, if peace is holistic, then it takes a multipronged strategy to protect it, and in some cases, avoidance can be the enemy of the peace you seek.

When you don't address the sin in your life, avoidance becomes the enemy of peace with God. When you hide from hard conversations in relationships, avoidance becomes the enemy of peace with people. When you don't deal with the trauma, unforgiveness, and bitterness plaguing your soul, avoidance becomes the enemy of inner peace. Instead of protecting your peace, skirting things you need to confront provides a pseudo-peace that is lost at the mere mention or thought of the situation or person you are dodging.

However, you protect your peace when you address the sin you are wrestling with, the relationships that need courageous conversations, or the impact of the trauma you've experienced. Friend, confrontation is hard. I get it. But don't avoid it, because peace is on the other side of the confrontation.

PEACE WITH OTHERS

As providence would have it, I saw Clark again a year later at a church conference; this time, I was more prepared. I had done the work in prayer and therapy and had processed much of the heartbreak within community. When Clark approached me, I was cordial. He asked if he could have a moment to speak with me, and with some hesitation, I agreed. I didn't know what he would say, so I listened. He apologized. And not just a general apology—he sincerely and thoroughly apologized for, in his words, "the layers of deception."

Surprised and thankful, I responded, "I forgive you."

"Thank you," Clark said.

We said goodbye; then I walked to my car. I shut the door, and an uncontrollable sob overcame me. Not because I was hurt but because I finally let it go.

I've run into Clark several times over the years since that apology, and we are always friendly. We can co-exist in the same space without tension. We no longer avoid each other, because we have peace.

When I did the work in prayer, therapy, and community, and when I finally let go and forgave Clark, I found a peace that can't be shaken. A peace that allows me to be around a source of trauma without being constantly triggered. A peace that surpasses all understanding.

Peace with others comes through the work we do in forgiveness and reconciliation. I was able to talk with and reconcile with Clark, but I recognize that sometimes those hard conversations aren't possible because of death, unrepentance on the offender's side, or the fact that it may be unsafe to be around the perpetrator.

The work of peace requires forgiveness.

However, the work of peace isn't limited to a courageous conversation. You can find peace with others by going to therapy to process your trauma, working through it with trusted friends and mentors, and processing with God in prayer and Bible reading. But above all, the work of peace requires forgiveness, and an apology isn't a prerequisite for that forgiveness.

FORGIVENESS AND JUSTICE

"Cancel the debt."

My eyes flew open, and I heard the words again: "Cancel the debt."

I lay in bed that Sunday morning and knew God was speaking to me. I also knew what He meant. I had been struggling to forgive a former friend, Tasha. After many years of supporting her, rarely asking for anything in return, I finally asked for our relationship to be more equitable and shared my concerns. Tasha declared that I was asking for too much and abruptly ended our friendship. I was baffled and hurt. I felt betrayed and used. Months afterward, my heart had grown bitter, and love had turned to hate. But here was God, asking me to forgive her.

I reminded Him of what she had done to me, hoping He would change His mind, but the answer was still the same: "Cancel the debt."

My heart reeled. I didn't want to forgive Tasha. "Lord, she hurt me. I want her to feel the same pain. I want justice!"

"Vengeance is Mine. I will repay. Cancel the debt," He told me.

Frustrated, I closed my eyes. Hoping to fall back to sleep, I couldn't shake the words that I had heard. "Why?" I questioned God. "She doesn't deserve it."

My desire for revenge was the biggest obstacle in canceling Tasha's debt. I wanted to balance the score, to get even. I had experienced injustice, and my heart longed for God to correct it—to give me justice—immediately. I didn't want her to get away with harming me.

Have you ever felt the same? Have you wanted revenge for an injustice done to you—a friend lied to you, a sibling betrayed you, a parent abandoned you—but God seems to be asleep at the wheel? Does He see or even know? Waiting on His vengeance can be frustrating and disorienting. Sometimes the people you want to experience God's vengeance may even seem to be experiencing His favor. How could He let this happen? I've been there, multiple times over. Yet when the frustration threatens to overwhelm, God gently reminds me of His deep love for everyone. As my dad always says, "God loves your enemies just as much as He loves you."

As I lay in bed, heart heavy with sorrow, God revealed that He was being patient and gracious with Tasha just like He had always been with me. While I appreciated God's grace toward me, I struggled when that same grace was extended to my enemies. I trusted God when He said, "Vengeance is Mine," but I wrestled with His timing. I couldn't speed up God's process or force His hand. He is sovereign. He does what He wants, when He wants, and how He wants. If I wanted His peace, then I had to surrender to it. I knew what I needed to do, even though I didn't want to: cancel the debt.

But night after night when I closed my eyes, the sting in my heart reminded me of the chasm between what I understood and how I felt. Nights turned into restless battles as I tried to command my heart to forgive, to let go.

One evening, the weight was too heavy. The pain was too raw and deep. I lay across my bed, knowing that I'd never be able to cancel this debt without God. I waved the white flag in my inner battle. "God," I whispered, tears trickling down my cheeks, "I can't do this on my own. If I'm ever going to forgive her, I need You to step in and heal my heart."

Friend, forgiveness is the only path to God's peace. Unless God grants you forgiveness, you can't have peace with Him, you can't maintain peace with people over time, and you can't have inner peace. Forgiveness is a crucial element. And like peace, it takes work.

During a sermon on forgiveness, Dr. Dharius Daniels once said that those who have offended us can never truly repay us. While I felt my friend owed me, she couldn't actually repay me. As Dr. Daniels would say, I had to "write [it] off as bad debt."[4] Even if she apologized, my friend couldn't give me back the days I spent being mad. She couldn't give me back the bad days that would have been good had she not hurt me. So I had to choose to cancel her debt, over and over again. Because forgiveness is an event and a process—a continual choice that we make, knowing we will never be repaid.

Jesus makes the same choice every time He forgives us of sin. He knows there is no way we can ever repay Him for the suffering He endured, so He just cancels the debt when we ask for forgiveness. Part of the reason I think God allows us to be offended by others is so we can feel a fraction of the weight of the offense our sin is to Him. When we compare the offenses done to us with the offenses He has experienced from us, we can understand His grace and mercy in a deeper way.

This deeper understanding of God's forgiveness softens our hearts and has two side effects. First, we become more willing to extend grace to others. When we extend forgiveness to those who offended us, we become a glimmer of the grace of God, a light that draws people closer to Him. The second side effect is that we are more open to areas in our own lives that need correction.

God is always looking for a two-for-one when dealing with people in relationships. He isn't just trying to correct the offender, but He is also looking to correct the offended. My therapist, Dr. Stacy, told me my former friend was like an agitator in a washing machine. The agitator is the part in the center that twists the clothes to remove dirt and stains. "You don't see it now, but God is using this offense as an agitator to purge some things out of you," she said.

If God allowed this agitation to happen, it was not for my destruction but for my development. Looking at the situation from that perspective shifted me from "God, why me?" to "God, what are You trying to show me through this?" When I stepped back and looked at it with fresh eyes, I could see that God wanted to purge some co-dependency and passive-aggressive tendencies out of me. I needed to learn how to address issues when they happened and not let them pile up. I needed to learn patience and how to love unconditionally. I needed to learn how to communicate better when I'm hurt. When I recognized what God was teaching me, I realized that my former friend wasn't the only one at fault for how the relationship had ended; I played a role too. I had been both a victim and a villain. That realization helped me get to compassion, and that helped me get to forgiveness, which led me to inner peace.

While my story is typical in relationships like friendships, marriage, and family, there are other cases in which offenses and injustices aren't at all the victim's fault. These cases include rape, abuse, assault, and exploitation of the marginalized by slavery, racism, and other unjust systems. In these cases, we are to be co-laborers with the Lord in the work of justice.

Dr. Martin Luther King, Jr., famously said, "True peace is not merely the absence of tension; it is the presence of justice."[5] You can't have peace in a world full of injustices without the pursuit of justice. In the face of the suffering and pain that unjust systems, abuse, exploitation, and marginalization create, we fight for justice with the knowledge that God's justice is now *and* not yet. That means that we fight on earth to get glimpses of the complete justice that will materialize on that great Day of Judgment when God will make all things right in heaven.

Please note that justice work doesn't exempt us from

forgiving. Forgiveness is the only way to do the work of justice from a pure heart and not a corrupt one. Forgiveness doesn't mean that God won't vindicate you or execute justice on your behalf, but it does mean that His timing and process won't paralyze you.

When I was young, my dad would preach in Panama City every year. Even though we were going for a revival, my parents would turn it into a mini family vacation. I would cram myself into the back seat with my two brothers, my parents in the front, excitement in my heart to be on a family trip. The only drawback was the drive from Jacksonville to Panama City. It was a little more than four hours, and I was miserable the whole ride.

I would constantly ask my dad how much farther we had to go. The more I asked, the slower time moved. While I was awake, counting the time, my mom would be sleeping. When we arrived, she would stretch and say, "We here already?" Whereas I would roll my eyes and whine, "Finally! That took forever." We had the same ride but two different experiences because she rested and I rushed it.

God's vengeance and justice are promises, but His timing requires patience. In the process of justice, forgiveness will move you from a state of rush to a state of rest. You can't rush God's timing, but you can have a better experience while waiting on Him. Trusting His timing will help give you the inner peace you long for.

INNER PEACE

Inner peace is a by-product of Christ's redemptive sacrifice and our own earnest efforts to maintain harmony with all. It's also born from a deliberate choice to not allow our anxieties to cloud our consciousness, to present them before God in prayer, and to be thankful for the abundant blessings we've already received. As Paul succinctly put it, "Don't worry about anything; instead, pray about everything. Tell God what you need, and thank him for all he has done. Then you will experience God's peace."[6] This peace is the fruit of a heart rooted in trust, dedicated to prayer, and filled with gratitude.

God has a perfect, holistic peace waiting for you. Friend, the road to peace is filled with many bumps and trials, but it's worth the trip. For when you do the work of peace and commit to prayer, rest will abide in your soul. The pain you feel will start to pass, and the peace that surpasses all understanding will settle over you. When you trust in God, then you can count on His promise:

You will keep in perfect peace
all who trust in you,
all whose thoughts are fixed on you![7]

PRAYER

God,

I am tormented by fear. I haven't experienced peace in a long time. My anxieties rob me of sleep, ruin my relationships, and keep me from experiencing an abundant life. I've tried everything to get peace, but nothing seems to work. I can't live like this any longer. I accept the work of peace that You have done and want to be in right relationship with You, Jesus. I want to do the work of peace, but forgiveness seems like an impossible task. I don't know how to release the debt. I honestly have no desire to be anywhere near the people who have hurt me. I need You to give me the desire for forgiveness and reconciliation.

Please give me the strength to do the work so I can finally experience Your peace. I'm honestly scared to face the things I've been running from. I need Your courage to have the conversations I need to have. Please help me forgive those I need to forgive. I can't do this on my own. I need You.

In Jesus's name, amen.

4

PROVISION

Truth is, I think, if God just gave us our daily
bread, many of us would be angry.

—FRANCIS CHAN

n February 2012, I started Jude 3 Project as a broke
seminary student. There was no start-up capital. I didn't
have a team and couldn't afford to pay for help, so I
learned how to do everything by myself. I created the
website with a Squarespace template and designed a logo
on a graphic app called Word Swag. After about a week,
I finalized and launched the website.

A few months later, Jude 3 Project hosted its first event
in a library auditorium in Jacksonville to help local pastors
better understand apologetics. There were almost thirty
pastors and other leaders in attendance. I was excited.

After two more events, I launched the *Jude 3 Project
Podcast.* On a whim, I decided to talk about Jay-Z's song

"Lost One" in relationship to the problem of evil. The podcast episode was less than fifteen minutes, and it was warmly received. I was onto something, so I contacted apologists and scholars via X (formerly Twitter) and email to secure guests for the podcast. To my surprise, most of them said yes. While I was thrilled about the podcast growth, I still had a problem: I needed money.

I reached out to the CEO of a national Christian non-profit I had met some years back to ask him for help with fundraising. I started the call excitedly, telling him all the growth I saw with the podcast and the website. I explained the need for contextualized apologetics in the Black community.

"I agree," he said. "But you have three things working against you: You're young, you're a woman, and you're Black."

My heart sank.

"The field of apologetics," he continued, "is dominated by older white men. It would be hard for you to gain traction."

At the end of the call, I was discouraged and wanted to quit. *God, You sent me on mission impossible. How am I ever going to get the resources I need?* I was anxious, frustrated, and hurt that God hadn't provided when He so clearly called me to this work. Even as I wrestled with whether He would supply the funds, I knew my struggle paled in comparison with not having basic needs met.

I once watched a video where a man lamented that his mom had given money to the church when they hadn't had any food at home. Can you imagine the pain and confusion that filled his heart every time his mom placed money in the collection plate when he knew that money could have stopped his hunger pains? His faith was completely shattered. He couldn't reconcile his mom's faithfulness to God with the poverty they continued to live in. For him, faith and church felt like a scam, and he wanted no part of it. I can only imagine how disorienting that had to be for him as a child and how that pain shaped his view of God and the church.

In college, my friend Tia went through a similar faith crisis. She came to faith in a prosperity-gospel-leaning church. In her mind and according to the prosperity theology she espoused, personal holiness, faithful giving, and consistent service in her church would grant her financial prosperity. Although Tia was a dedicated believer and served her church, she experienced a series of unfortunate events that deeply affected her bank account. She struggled with basic needs like food and housing. She couldn't reconcile what she was experiencing in life with the prosperity theology that her church taught. Tia was forced to deal with the fallout of a works-based faith. Pain permeated her life and led her to a dark place where she started questioning everything.

Many, like Tia, struggle because they were given a false reality. God's provision—the supplying of a need—didn't meet their expectations. They read Paul's words when he told the church at Philippi that God would supply all their needs.[1] So they expected that, because they are God's children, God would meet every need they had. If He is the one who is supposed to be taking care of them and they don't have their needs met, then are His other promises still true? Can they trust His love, knowledge, and ability? God's lack of provision becomes a pain point when we hear the wrong information about His promises, and it intensifies when we are also on the margins.

One of my favorite scriptures is Psalm 73. The psalmist Asaph declared,

> I almost lost my footing.
>   My feet were slipping, and I was almost gone.
> For I envied the proud
>   when I saw them prosper despite their wickedness.
> They seem to live such painless lives;
>   their bodies are so healthy and strong.
> They don't have troubles like other people;
>   they're not plagued with problems like everyone else.[2]

Nothing challenges our views on God and faith more than seeing people who are evil with provision and those on the margins pursuing God without. At the crux of

Asaph's frustration was the same pain point. He almost lost his faith observing the prosperity of the wicked. How, then, do we make sense of God's provision? What should be our expectations?

GOD'S GOOD GIFTS

In the northern kingdom of Israel during the time of King Ahab, there lived a prophet, Elijah. God spoke through Elijah and performed great miracles through him. In a nearby town, there lived a poor widow who had no one to provide for her. At that time, there was a drought in the land and food was scarce for everyone.

God led the prophet to the widow, and Elijah asked her to provide for him. The widow told him that all she had was a little flour and some cooking oil. She was going to use these meager supplies to prepare one final meal for her and her son. Without hesitation, Elijah responded that God would provide for the woman and her son if she made food for him first. I can imagine her son feeling like the man in the video: "Why would we give our last food to a prophet when we don't have any other food to eat?" However, the woman did what Elijah said, and her containers never ran out of flour and oil. God provided.[3]

If I could sit down with the man in the video, the one

who feels faith failed him, I would listen intently and lament the times he felt God let him down. I can't pretend to know the sting of hunger while watching your mom give her last few dollars instead of buying you a meal. Yet the very fact that he's here, sharing his story, tells me that, in some mysterious way, God provided for him.

God knows every need we have, whether it be food, clothing, or shelter. These needs can cause us great anxiety, frustration, and pain when we don't know how they will be met. However, God's prescription for the pain that comes with the lack of provision is the command to not worry. Jesus said, "Don't worry about these things, saying, 'What will we eat? What will we drink? What will we wear?' These things dominate the thoughts of unbelievers, but your heavenly Father already knows all your needs. Seek the Kingdom of God above all else, and live righteously, and he will give you everything you need."[4]

But how can you not worry when the problem is staring you in the face? How can you not feel crushed when you have more bills than money? How can you have peace when you hear your child's stomach growling and your bank account is in the negative?

Friend, you can have faith in God's provision for you because you are precious to Him. If God sent His only Son to die for you, then you can trust that He will also provide for you. He loves you more than you could ever imagine. Like the faithful Father He is, God wants good things for you. Jesus reminded us of God's goodness and love when He said, "You parents—if your children ask for a loaf of bread, do you give them a stone instead? Or if they ask for a fish, do you give them a snake? Of course not! So if you sinful people know how to give good gifts to your children, how much more will your heavenly Father give good gifts to those who ask him."[5]

God wants to provide for you—and God will provide for you—because He loves you. He sees you and He is for you. Even when systems plot against you, God is fighting for you.

PROVISION AND THE MARGINALIZED

In a viral YouTube clip, activist and psychologist Dr. Umar Johnson argued that Christianity keeps Black people in a perpetual state of servitude and strips us of our monetary resources through tithes and offerings with no return on our investment. His clear implication is that Black churches don't do enough to empower Black communities. He even argued that Black churches actually help white people destroy Black neighborhoods.[6]

Dr. Johnson continues to argue his point even though tons of historical evidence refute this claim. Here are a few examples: Black churches started credit unions to help Black people obtain loans when traditional banks turned them away. Black churches helped create Historically Black Colleges and Universities to educate and empower Black people. And Black churches played a major role in the civil rights movement.[7] His mischaracterization of Black churches has grieved me, but I understand the frustration behind his argument.

He is rightfully brokenhearted by the often-overlooked disparities in Black communities. I can understand his anger when the oversimplified solution given by some who benefit off the backs of the marginalized is to wait for a better life in heaven, even though they could help make Black people's lives economically better on earth. Those feelings are valid and warranted. Black people have experienced and are experiencing injustice in America, and we must speak against it. We can take courage in speaking against what God also has spoken against throughout Scripture. God is very clear on His posture toward the marginalized and injustice:

Never take advantage of poor and destitute laborers, whether they are fellow Israelites or foreigners living in your towns.[8]

Don't rob the poor just because you can,
or exploit the needy in court.

For the Lord is their defender.

He will ruin anyone who ruins them.[9]

The godly care about the rights of the poor;

the wicked don't care at all.[10]

Their houses are full of deceit;
they have become rich and powerful

and have grown fat and sleek.
Their evil deeds have no limit;

they do not seek justice.
They do not promote the case of the fatherless;

they do not defend the just cause of the poor.[11]

I want to see a mighty flood of justice,

an endless river of righteous living.[12]

Pure and genuine religion in the sight of God the Father means caring for orphans and widows in their distress and refusing to let the world corrupt you.[13]

God is just, and He is bothered and angered by injustice. He knows the feeling of being treated unjustly. He came to earth to save His creation, and they killed Him. Friend, God can identify with every injustice you feel. He can sympa-

God is just, and He is bothered and angered by injustice.

thize with your frustrations. While He can sympathize with your grievances, He also wants you to know that He will make all the injustices right. His justice is a reminder that He sees, knows, and cares for you and that He will provide for you. He may not provide in the way you think He should, but He will make sure all your needs are met.

UNLIKELY SOURCES

A few years into Jude 3 Project, I built a relationship with a large Christian organization. I had been deeply shaped by their ministry. I was honored that they had noticed my work and taken a liking to me. After I engaged with their team for almost a year, one of their vice presidents requested a meeting with me. He knew that we were financially struggling as a small organization, so he made me a nice offer.

He said I could bring Jude 3 Project under their organization and I wouldn't have to worry about money. They would pay my salary and give me access to all their resources. I was thankful for the offer, but I declined. If Jude 3 Project was going to fulfill its mission, then it would need to stay independent. Being tethered to a majority white Christian organization would work against us.

"I understand," he said. "How much seed funding would you need?"

I responded, "Around $350,000."

He chuckled and said, "That's it? I can raise that for you in one phone call." Just when I was about to get excited, he continued, "I need to get to know you better first. Let's revisit this in a year."

My heart dropped. I felt so defeated. I didn't think I had another year to wait if I wanted Jude 3 Project to stay afloat. He could have helped me with one phone call, but he didn't. I left the office thinking, *So you know me well enough to take it from me but not well enough to empower me with resources to continue it on my own.*

I was crushed and disappointed because someone who could have helped didn't. He had dangled a carrot and yanked it back. However, while reading 1 Kings, I was reminded that God's provision can come through unlikely sources.

God provided for the prophet Elijah in an unlikely way—a widow fed him. God could have used other people or other resources that would have made more sense to Elijah, but God chose the unlikely. Sometimes, if He provided through the logical source, we might be tempted to give credit to the person who helped us, but when He provides in unconventional ways, all glory goes to Him.

The organization's vice president didn't get me the

resources I needed—he was the likely source. Instead, someone on a lower level in the company—an unlikely provider—fought to get help for me. While it wasn't the total amount, the money he did give made a significant difference. I had assumed he couldn't help me because he didn't have the power I thought was needed to make the call. He may not have been the vice president, but God used his influence to get me the help I needed.

Has the Lord shown up for you when you least expected it? Has He used an unlikely person to provide for you? Think hard, because sometimes you won't even realize He has done it until you look back with a new perspective.

A FRESH OUTLOOK

When I was working to get Jude 3 Project off the ground, it was difficult to ignore how different the start-up process seemed for my white colleagues who had similar endeavors. Raising money came easier for them, and they didn't have to face the obstacles I do as a Black female apologist in America. When they raised money, the formula was already laid out: Go to the people with wealth in your network, share your vision with them, and ask them for a major gift. That was never my experience. I didn't have that kind of network. Instead, I had to overcome racial and gender biases and find new ways to raise money for our mission. Honestly, I resented God for the fundraising challenges I endured—until the pandemic.

While many of my colleagues struggled because they relied on old fundraising and programming models that wouldn't work during the pandemic, Jude 3 Project grew in influence and revenue. Before the pandemic, I had learned new ways to sustain our organization through products, services, and innovative fundraising. I had already navigated the turmoil and learned how to depend on God to survive.

My friend BJ jokingly said that I was already prepared for the pandemic because I was in a financial pandemic before the pandemic. He's right. Because of the struggle I endured, I learned to trust in the Lord while others trusted in their own ability and resources. The whole time I was resenting God for the hardships, He was preparing me to weather a giant storm.

God is preparing you for the storms you will face. Remember all the things you've experienced that you thought you weren't going to overcome? Now what seemed like impossible situations have turned into miraculous testimonies. Remember when you prayed for a job and God provided one? Remember when you didn't know how you were going to pay rent but somehow you were able to pay it? Remember when you could barely afford the dollar menu at McDonald's and God provided?

Every storm you've weathered has prepared you to trust God for your present needs. You have too much experience with God to give up on Him now. Storms are means that He uses to grow us. I don't like this reality, but this is how He has chosen to do it. "Dear brothers and sisters, when troubles of any kind come your way, consider it an opportunity for great joy. For you know that when your faith is tested, your endurance has a chance to grow. So let it grow, for when your endurance is fully developed, you will be perfect and complete, needing nothing."[14] God wants to equip you to endure the hardships you will face. You may not be able to see what He is doing now, but it will all make sense when you look back some time from now.

HIS TIMING, NOT OURS

Our first national conference for Jude 3 Project was a leap of faith. By all accounts, I shouldn't have been planning a conference. We didn't have any money as an organization; we didn't have a team. I had no connections, no prior experience; all I had was a word from God that, if I'm honest, I wasn't sure about. To pull the conference off, it would take more than $50,000. I had never raised that much for an event in my life. To make matters worse, I had to do it in four months.

I created a sponsorship packet and sent it to everyone and everywhere: to corporations, seminaries, universities, publishers, and so on. I couldn't get anyone to bite. Time was running out. I had already booked hotel conference rooms and signed speaker contracts, but I had raised only $2,500 in one month. I was stressed out of my mind and was on the verge of depression.

Just when I was about to give up, I received a call from a friend attending a well-known seminary. He said his dean was on vacation with his family in Jacksonville and wanted to meet with me. I was hesitant; I didn't want to go to another meeting. I just wanted to lie in bed and sulk. Reluctantly, I went to dinner.

While I was with the dean and his family, he said, "I've been advocating for you on campus, and I think I can get you $10,000 for your conference."

My mouth almost dropped open. I had never met this man before, but God was using him as a champion for me on his campus. His advocacy worked, and his school gave us $10,000 for the conference.

When I received the check, my heart soared. I had been working tirelessly and had raised only $2,500, but God had been working behind the scenes to provide for me from an unlikely source. Now, I would have liked God to provide all the money I needed in the first week of fundraising, but that wasn't how He decided to do it. As my friend Mike says, "God is one for dramatics." It wasn't the time I would have chosen, but it was on time. When the conference rolled around, we had everything we needed. God provided.

Has that ever happened to you? Has God ever provided for you when you were on the verge of giving up? Have you ever received an unexpected check in the mail? Have you ever been awarded a scholarship that you didn't even know you were qualified for? Have you ever been given a raise that you didn't request? God loves to flex His strength in unexpected ways, in His timing, for His glory. I've seen Him do it for me, and I've also witnessed Him do it for others.

Trina and Angelo, dear friends of mine, were struggling financially. Angelo was a business owner, and Trina was a stay-at-home mom. The economy had taken a toll on Angelo's business, and to stay afloat, they maxed out all their credit cards. Trina and Angelo were now in danger of losing everything. They were attempting to find side jobs to make some extra income, but they weren't having any luck. Everything was falling apart. The situation got worse by the day. They had no money for rent, food, or car payments. They were both stressed and frustrated. All they knew to do was seek God. So they began to pray and fast. Over the next month, people at their church randomly gave to them, without even knowing their situation. By the end of the month, God had provided everything the couple needed.

I would have loved for God to provide for them when they first asked or miraculously made Angelo's business prosper, but God chose to bless them in His way and in His timing. I've seen His perfect timing play out in my life, the life of this dear couple, and also the life of Peter, a disciple of Jesus.

Before Peter was a disciple, he was a fisherman. In the book of Luke, we meet Peter after a long night of fishing, struggling because he'd caught nothing. Fishing was how he provided for himself and his family, so imagine how disheartened he would have been to spend a night at work with no payment. Enter Jesus. As Peter was getting ready to quit for the day, Jesus told him to try again. He reluctantly obliged and cast his nets into the lake—the same nets he'd used and the same lake he'd fished in *all night*. Yet in Jesus's timing, Peter caught so many fish that his nets broke.[15]

God could have provided fish for Peter when he first let down his nets, but He waited until later because He had a purpose. He used the delay so Peter could see the miraculous power Jesus possessed. That power drew Peter to Jesus and led to his discipleship. God's delay was purposeful.

Like Peter, I drew closer to Jesus in my provision crisis before the Jude 3 Project conference. Angelo and Trina's financial woes allowed them to see a new side of God and has drawn them closer to Him too. Every delay of provision taught us something new about God that we wouldn't have learned if He had been working on our timeline.

Friend, when you realize God is working behind the scenes, you will be more content with His timing; you will trust that He will do what He said: provide every need. The old folks in church used to say, "He may not come when you want Him, but He is always on time." God's timing is something to be grateful for. His timing is a promise you can trust in.

GRATEFUL HEARTS

When the children of Israel escaped Egypt, they were led into the wilderness—a dry and unforgiving environment. While they were there, God provided for them. He gave them manna—bread from heaven—that supplied all their dietary needs, and He ensured their clothes didn't wear out. He was meeting their needs but not their desires.

After a time, the Israelites forgot how brutal slavery was in Egypt. They recalled the few things they had enjoyed, especially the meat. They desired the meat from Egypt. The people compared God's provision—manna—with the meat they craved, and they lost their gratitude for all He had done.[16]

Comparison steals gratitude. When the children of Israel compared meat and manna, they lost their ability to be grateful. They couldn't see the blessings God had heaped on them, from food and water to shelter, guidance, freedom, and more. If we're honest, we can admit we easily fall into the same comparison trap as the Israelites. When we compare God's provision with our unmet desires, we lose gratitude. When we lose gratitude, we lose the ability to see all the ways God has provided for us.

Has God provided in your time of need, even if it didn't meet your desires? Have you ever become ungrateful when He didn't meet your needs the way you wanted Him to? What would happen if instead of seeing the gap between our desires and needs, we saw the blessings God gave us? What if instead of being angry about not receiving a new car, we saw the blessing of the free bus pass He sent? What if we thanked God for the leftover pizza from work that we could take home for our children to eat? How loudly would our hearts sing if we saw the blessing in every gift?

The next time you're on your knees, begging God for provision, ask Him for eyes to see the blessings, the unlikely provision. Ask Him to shield your heart from comparing what you want with what you need. Ask Him for gratitude. When you do, He will open your eyes, and your trust in Him and His provision will grow.

PAY IT FORWARD

On December 10, 1979, Mother Teresa accepted the Nobel Peace Prize in Norway. In her acceptance speech, she told a story that I will never forget:

> One evening a gentleman came to our house and said, there is a Hindu family and the eight children have not eaten for a long time. Do something for them. And I took rice and I went immediately. [The] mother . . . took the rice from my hand, she divided into two and she went out. When she came back, I asked her, where did you go? What did you do? And one answer she gave me: They are hungry also. She knew that the next door neighbor, a Muslim family, was hungry.[17]

I'm always deeply convicted by this part of Mother Teresa's speech. Honestly, I'm not sure splitting the rice would have been my first instinct. However, this woman didn't care only about herself and her family; she also cared about her neighbor. This woman knew that provision is to be shared. God blesses us to be a blessing to others. Paul told the church at Corinth, "God gives seed to farmers and provides everyone with food. He will increase what you have, so you can give even more to those in need. You will be blessed in every way, and you will be able to keep on being generous. Then many people will thank God when we deliver your gift."[18] Provision is His work and ours.

A few years ago, I was in line at Starbucks getting my favorite drink, an iced caramel macchiato, after a long and stressful day. I pulled up to the window to pay, and to my surprise, the car in front of me had already paid for mine. I smiled, said "Thank you," and drove off.

On the way home, my friend called me. I told her my day was rough but there was a silver lining. The person in front of me paid for my drink at Starbucks.

She asked me, "So did you pay it forward?"

I responded, "No."

She said, "Lisa, you were supposed to pay for the person behind you to keep it going."

I sighed. "I was so focused on how stressful my day had been that I didn't even think of it."

Our problems have a way of blinding us to the blessing God has called us to be. Blessings shouldn't stop with us; they should flow through us. That flow is the way God works to meet people's needs. We are channels of God's provision.

Jesus put weight on our responsibility to be His channels of provision for people around us. He said that if you haven't done it for those in need, you haven't done it for Him:

"I was hungry and you gave me nothing to eat, I was thirsty and you gave me nothing to drink, I was a stranger and you did not invite me in, I needed clothes and you did not clothe me, I was sick and in prison and you did not look after me."

They also will answer, "Lord, when did we see you hungry or thirsty or a stranger or needing clothes or sick or in prison, and did not help you?"

He will reply, "Truly I tell you, whatever you did not do for one of the least of these, you did not do for me."[19]

Friend, provision isn't just God's job; it's your job. When you're unwilling to be a channel, you create eternal consequences for yourself. In fact, Matthew recorded that Jesus said those who don't care for people on the margins will hear God say these words: "Depart from me, you who are cursed."[20] However, when you care for the needs you see, you honor God.

The day after my failure at Starbucks, I went back. My friend's words were ringing in my ears, so I paid for the person in line behind me. Nothing had changed in my life. I was still facing complicated situations, but I knew that should never prevent me from being a blessing to someone else.

Your part in provision isn't just about picking up the tab for strangers at Starbucks. How much you've been

given determines your role in provision: "When someone has been entrusted with much, even more will be
required."[21] The more you receive, the more you're required to provide.

However, your part in provision isn't limited to in-
creased giving. If how you obtain wealth perpetuates the
cycles of poverty that you donate to alleviate, then you
work against God's intention. You're responsible for assessing the sources of your revenue to ensure how you
make money doesn't create systems of poverty and disparities for others.

George Whitefield was an Anglican priest at the helm
of one of the greatest revivals in history, the Great Awak-
ening. Whitefield was a complicated preacher. While he
was passionate about spreading the gospel message and
founding orphanages, he was a proponent of slavery and
he enslaved people himself. Whitefield started orphanages to provide food and shelter for fatherless and mother-
less children while at the same time advocating for an
oppressive system of slavery that separated Black parents
from children. He was both helping to create orphans and
helping to create places to care for orphans.

As egregious as Whitefield's duplicity is, if your wealth
is built on the marginalization of others, then your actions
are just as atrocious. Giving yourself a pass for contribut-
ing to an oppressive system because you give to charity is
hypocritical. One of the most common ways this plays

out today is through gentrification. Gentrification is "a process in which a poor area (as of a city) experiences an influx of middle-class or wealthy people who renovate and rebuild homes and businesses and which often results in an increase in property values and the displacement of earlier, usually poorer residents."[22] Gentrification has affected every major city in America and displaced countless Black and Brown people. Many middle-class or wealthy people who live in gentrified areas may pride themselves on giving to charity to help those on the margins, but they often miss that their decision to move to gentrified areas has left many homeless. Providing for the needy *and* assessing the systems that create need are at the core of economic justice—and important pieces of our part in God's will and provision.

In the Bible, we read about a wealthy tax collector named Zacchaeus. As a tax collector, he took extra money from the poor to promote his wealthy lifestyle. However, when Jesus passed through Jericho, Zacchaeus had a life-changing encounter and repented of his evil ways. But he didn't stop there. His repentance stretched beyond lip service into action.

Zacchaeus understood that he was part of an oppressive system that exploited those on the margins. He knew that it wasn't enough to leave the system without assessing the damage he had done and doing the repair work. So he vowed, "Here and now I give half of my possessions to the poor, and if I have cheated anybody out of anything, I will pay back four times the amount."[23]

Friend, God is calling you to first evaluate whether you're a part of the problem you're trying to solve. Then He is asking you to do the work of repair. That, too, is part of His provision. If you've been given much, then you have the awesome opportunity to alleviate some of the pain of others when you meet them in the gap between their lack and your abundance. You can be a part of God's provision and healing for His people.

PRAYER

God,

I'm frustrated with my current financial space. I know You provide, but sometimes it doesn't feel like it. Sometimes life seems to get worse, not better. I'm trying to believe in Your faithfulness, but my bills tell me a different story.

Help me trust in Your justice when I'm facing unjust economic systems. Help me trust that You will provide for me in Your timing, even if it's through unlikely sources. Remind me of all the ways You have provided for me in the past. Open my eyes to Your blessings in my life right now. Give me a fresh outlook to see how You are working these things together for my good and Your glory. Forgive me for complaining when You didn't provide the way I wanted You to.

Give me a heart of compassion when You do provide so I can be a blessing to others.

In Jesus's name, amen.

5

PLEASURE

Now I have it all, and I feel empty inside.
—TARAJI HENSON, interview on
America in Black on BET

few years ago, I met with Stanley, who had been part of my undergrad campus ministry. He had recently left the Christian faith but wanted to meet with me to discuss his choice. At first, it seemed his biggest complaint was the idea of hell. He couldn't accept that a loving God would send people to eternal torment. But soon he moved to his challenges with science and the Bible. Just when I thought I understood his main issues with the faith, he would move to another concern. He jumped from subject to subject with ease. I didn't respond; I just listened.

About four hours later, we got to the root of his rejection of Christianity. To my surprise, it wasn't hell or science; it was the idea of sexual morality. He wanted to have premarital sex with no consequences or condemnation. He no longer wanted to be bound to the biblical restrictions around sex; he wanted to be free to experience unrestricted pleasure.

If we're honest, unrestricted pleasure without consequences sounds like an amazing idea on the surface. Your desire may not look exactly like Stanley's, but maybe you would love to eat as many cookies, cakes, and pies as you wanted without gaining any weight or spend your whole life on vacation without worrying about work. While these lifestyles sound nice, they are far from reality. We live in a world bound by rules, and every choice has consequences. If we eat too many cakes, our clothes no longer fit. If we take too much time off, we may be out of a job.

While unrestricted pleasure can lead to problems, pleasure in and of itself isn't good or bad; it's neutral. Pleasure is simply the feeling of happiness or enjoyment produced by a particular activity. That definition alone seems to make pleasure inconsequential.

You may be thinking, *If pleasure is simply enjoyment and happiness, why would God place restrictions on it? Doesn't He want me to be happy and enjoy life? Hasn't He come to give us life more abundantly? Why would pleasure need limitations? Isn't joy a fruit of the Spirit?*

If you think God's will is solely about your happiness and enjoyment, I can imagine that the Christian faith has been a big disappointment for you. You probably sometimes feel like you had more happiness without Christ than you have with Him. The joy that you thought He provides keeps evading your doorstep. In fact, it seems like since you accepted Christ, your life has actually gotten worse.

God was supposed to heal the pain, not create more. So you had to take matters into your own hands, pursuing pleasure to heal the pain. If God wouldn't do it, you had to do it yourself. However, even when you take matters into your own hands, you still are at war with the pain.

The pursuit of pleasure without God will leave you empty.

Friend, happiness can't heal you. Pleasure isn't the cure for pain. It can make you feel better momentarily, but it doesn't have the power to heal the deep wounds of the soul. The pursuit of pleasure without God will leave you empty.

EMPTY PLEASURE

For many years, I pursued pleasure through my achievements. I worked hard at school and focused on graduating from college because I thought it would make me happy. When I finally graduated, I was happy, but it didn't last long. I started looking for the next happiness fix: getting my desired salary, buying my dream car, growing a strong platform. Nothing made me happy. So I decided to focus on Jude 3 Project. If I could just get my non-profit to succeed, then I'd be happy because I'd be making a difference. Right?

I worked tirelessly through the pandemic, producing content nonstop. I flew across the country, fundraising and speaking at conferences. Jude 3 Project released two documentaries and hosted several events. I was all over the place. In 2022, Jude 3 Project experienced significant growth, and we continued to grow, reaching milestone after milestone, but I was tired and unhappy. All the achievements I thought would bring me joy gave me only momentary satisfaction. Happiness was fleeting, and I was empty.

In Ecclesiastes, King Solomon described the emptiness I was feeling: "Anything I wanted, I would take. I denied myself no pleasure. I even found great pleasure in hard work, a reward for all my labors. But as I looked at everything I had worked so hard to accomplish, it was all so meaningless—like chasing the wind. There was nothing really worthwhile anywhere."[1] He was expressing what I felt, what so many of my peers have felt when they fell into the pleasure trap: an empty pleasure that led to great pain and depression.

I learned the hard way what the famous actor Jim Carrey once stated: "I wish people could realize all their dreams and wealth and fame so that they could see that it's not where you're going to find your sense of completion."[2] Pleasure in itself isn't enough to satisfy us.

Yet once we know that empty pleasure, then what? Where do we go from there? Can pleasure ever measure up to our expectations? And once we find something that brings us happiness, how do we determine whether what feels good to us is good *for* us? How do we distinguish between right and wrong pleasure? Should we evaluate it by the harm it does to others? Can we label it good pleasure if it doesn't harm anyone and brings us happiness? What is the rubric?

DO WHAT MAKES YOU HAPPY

A quick scroll on social media reveals a pervasive message across memes, posts, and videos: "Do what feels good as long as it doesn't harm anyone else." In fact, as I'm writing this book, there are more than three hundred million videos on TikTok with the hashtag #DoWhatMakes YouHappy. For many, the metric for whether you should or shouldn't do something—endlessly scroll on Instagram, party, binge-watch your favorite Netflix series—is how it makes you feel and who it harms. But is this a helpful rubric? And if it isn't, then what is the rubric we should be following?

When God created man and woman in the beginning, He gave them one restriction: not to eat from the tree of the knowledge of good and evil.[3] He gave them free rein in the garden; the only thing that was off-limits was that tree. Despite everything they had access to, Adam and Eve were tempted by a serpent to eat fruit from the forbidden tree. Once they both ate the fruit, sin entered the world and they saw themselves and the world differently. It seems so inconsequential. What can be wrong with fruit? Can all the chaos, death, and injustice we experience really have come because someone ate fruit?

Honestly, it feels like a gross overreaction to their breaking a seemingly small command. I mean, who got hurt by Adam and Eve eating fruit? There was no one on earth but them. What was wrong with them taking the fruit if it made them happy? It wasn't like they were cheating on each other, killing each other, or robbing each other. It was small; this was fruit.

However, while it seems minor, any violation of God's commands is a big deal because He is holy—"distinct from anything that has ever existed or will ever exist . . . entirely morally pure."[4] The prophet Isaiah testified that heavenly creatures called seraphim flew around God's throne, crying out,

Holy, holy, holy is the LORD of hosts;
the whole earth is full of his glory![5]

The seraphim said "holy" three times to emphasize how distinct God's nature is—there is no one in the universe like Him.

Because of His holiness, everything God commands is right and just. He is the only one with all knowledge and power, and therefore, He gets to determine what rules we should follow. Eating fruit was a problem for Adam and Eve only because God told them not to eat it. The metric for right or wrong wasn't who it harmed or how it felt; the metric was what God commanded. God possesses the wholly good and just character needed to create the guidelines for us, His creation. We were created to live inside His rules for pleasure. When we operate outside those guidelines, we are living outside His design.

My favorite card game is Uno. During my childhood summers, my cousins and I would play Uno all day at my grandparents' house. We never read the directions on the box; we made up our own rules. Our favorite variations to play with were "triples and doubles" and "train." In this style of play, you could go out in one turn.

Triples and doubles meant you could put down two or three of the same card in a single turn—yes, that included the Reverse, Skip, Wild, and Draw cards. Train meant you were allowed to play multiple cards if they fell in ascending or descending order. We wanted to play only by these rules. We weren't interested in the instructions that the creators of Uno put on the box. We had fun playing the game our way.

A few years ago, Uno's official X (formerly Twitter) account started tweeting the game rules; many people revolted, and some even responded that the official Uno account didn't know how to play its own game. I chuckled as I read the replies, because I slightly agreed. How the official Uno account instructed us to play felt tedious. I wanted to play it my way. My way worked for me, my way was fun, but my way wasn't how the game was designed to be played. While I could get pleasure from the game, I was operating outside its creators' design.

Similarly, God has designed us with a purpose in mind. Because of that, He gives instructions for every part of our lives. How we live matters to Him. His instructions include everything from how much we eat to who we sleep with. We may have fun living outside His commands and even enjoy our way more (like me with Uno), but we will never be able to follow His intention for our lives if we live outside His guidelines for pleasure.

WHY WOULD GOD RESTRICT US?

When God created the Garden of Eden, He called everything good. All the animals, the grass, the people, the trees—everything was good. But if everything was good, then why did He instruct Adam and Eve not to eat from a particular tree? Could it be that just because something is good doesn't mean it's good for us?

My friends and I went to Raleigh for a conference several years ago. On our way back home, we stopped at a restaurant. While at the table, one of my friends offered us all hand sanitizer, and I quickly obliged. As soon as I put it on, I began to itch. I looked at the label and ran to the bathroom to wash my hands. When I returned, my friends asked me what was wrong. I explained to them that I'm allergic to all Bath & Body Works products. When I applied hand sanitizer without reading the label, I didn't realize it was the brand I'm allergic to, but the immediate effects were the signal. Nothing was inherently wrong with the hand sanitizer, but it wasn't good for me.

Good things can harm us. God told Adam and Eve not to eat of the tree—not to keep them from experiencing pleasure but for their protection. His instructions are designed to protect us in this game called life. And unlike playing by my own Uno rules, when we live outside God's design, the consequences are serious.

While at the graveside for my great-uncle's funeral several years ago, I overheard two men talking. One gentleman looked at the other and said, "You know, as soon as we are born, we start to die." When I think of Adam and

Eve, I think of this statement because as soon as they ate the fruit, as soon as they sinned, they started dying.

Friend, the fruit of sin—living outside God's design—is death. It rots our souls and suffocates our very being. However, sin's effects aren't always immediate. That is part of the deceptive nature of sin. Over time, you can convince yourself that it isn't corrosive, because there were no instant effects, but in the words of Emanuel Lambert, aka Da' T.R.U.T.H., "Just cause judgment ain't sudden don't mean that it ain't coming."[6]

God wanted Adam and Eve to experience pleasure. We know this because He gave them an entire garden and each other to enjoy. But He also wanted to protect them from the things that would harm them—the sin that only He, as an all-knowing being, could see coming. Adam and Eve had no idea that they would unlock sin, death, and chaos through one act of disobedience. All they saw was their pleasure. They were unaware of the consequences that would follow. So God restricted them from eating the fruit. He called the tree and everything else He made "good," but the tree in the middle of the garden wasn't good *for* Adam and Eve.

Likewise, God restricts us from some pleasures that He created because, in His wisdom, He knows that not all good things are good for us. His restrictions are always His protection. They often seem unnecessary at first glance. However, there are no restrictions without reasons. G. K. Chesterton gave a poignant illustration of this principle:

> There exists in such a case a certain institution or law; let us say, for the sake of simplicity, a fence or gate erected across a road. The more modern type of reformer goes gaily up to it and says, "I don't see the use of this; let us clear it away." To which the more intelligent type of reformer will do well to answer: "If you don't see the use of it, I certainly won't let you clear it away. Go away and think. Then, when you can come back and tell me that you *do* see the use of it, I may allow you to destroy it."[7]

Chesterton's quote reminds us that before we remove something, we should figure out why the restriction was there in the first place. What fences has God put around your pursuit of pleasure? What boundaries has He given that you find hard not to violate? Those are the weak areas in your life that the Enemy will try to exploit.

The Enemy will use the same tricks to deceive you that he used in the garden. He will ask you questions like "Is this really wrong?" "Did God really say?" or "Who is this really hurting?" because he wants you to second-guess God's instructions and intentions. Satan seeks opportunities to kill, steal, and destroy,[8] so he feeds you questions about the goodness of God.

Satan wants to turn you against the One who is protecting you. He wants to convince you that God's reasons aren't good. Because if you don't think God wants good for you, then how can you trust that His decisions are good? How can you know that He has His best in store for you? Your view of God's intentions will determine how much you follow His restrictions on pleasure. If you don't think God has your good in mind, then you will pursue pleasure on your terms.

BALANCING THE SCALES

"I resent God," I said. I was talking with my therapist, and the words ran out of my mouth before I could catch them.

"Why?" she asked.

"It seems like God is only interested in using me to help other people through Jude 3 Project. Or He helps with other ministry opportunities because they fit into His plan, but He isn't interested in granting me the desires of my heart in other areas of my life. I haven't met a husband yet, I am still navigating challenging friendships, and I haven't reached my financial goals. Those prayers seem to be overlooked by God. But He answers almost anything related to Jude 3 Project. I resent the call of ministry in my life. I'm drained. Burned out.

Everything feels like work. I don't want to do it any-more."

I had given my all to Jude 3 Project. My nights, my weekends, my sleep, my heart—everything. Yet I felt like God hadn't poured back into me. The scales of work ver-sus pleasure were unbalanced. Surely the Master of the Universe had seen my unhappiness. Did that mean the God who sees my heart and all its desires had chosen to remain quiet? Didn't I deserve happiness after all my hard work?

If God won't balance the scales, then I will.

So I looked for pleasure in the easiest form I could: food. I would eat whatever I wanted to boost my endor-phins and feel happy. I had pasta, bread pudding, steaks, milkshakes, and more. Any measure of delicious food I could find to treat myself for a job well done. I balanced the scales.

Can you relate? Have you been weighed down by the world and felt the lack of pleasure in your life? Have you sought out a vice to help balance the scales? Perhaps, like me, you turned to food. Or perhaps you sought pleasure with porn, drugs, or social media. Our vices aim to find happiness amid the pain. While some vices are sinful, others are inherently good things that have been overused and are now idols for us.

Remember, pleasure is neutral; it's neither good nor bad. However, the vehicle we use to get to pleasure determines the adjective that precedes it. When we pursue pleasure outside God's design, it brings adverse side effects.

I've noticed that during almost every television show, there is a commercial advertising a new medical drug to treat an illness. I'm always perplexed when they list possible side effects because there seem to be more negative side effects than benefits. Wouldn't it be devastating if you took medicine to alleviate headaches but it ended up causing blood clots? While drugs take away problems, they create others. This isn't just true about drugs; it's also true about pleasure.

When we pursue pleasure on our terms, we end up with unexpected side effects. For me, the side effect of my overeating was weight gain; because of that, I no longer liked how I looked, which had an impact on my self-esteem. If you've tried to use pleasure to offset the pain, your side effects may vary. Sex outside marriage can lead to sexually transmitted diseases (STDs), unwanted pregnancy, and guilt. Mindless online scrolling can lead to envy and insecurity. And stress eating can lead to health challenges, shame, and low self-esteem. Some pleasures create cycles of addiction and strongholds in our lives. Our uninhibited pursuit of pleasure creates problems, not solutions, leaving the scales unbalanced. We can never balance the scales; only God can do that because His pleasures don't have adverse side effects: "The blessing of the LORD, it maketh rich, and he addeth no sorrow with it."[9]

GOD'S PLEASURE

God isn't interested in withholding all pleasure from us on earth. In fact, He has come for us to have life and have it abundantly.[10] He wants us to have joy. He wants us to experience laughter. He wants us to enjoy sex within the context He ordained. He wants us to enjoy life. The Garden of Eden is proof of that.

God gave Adam and Eve everything to enjoy. His idea from the beginning was for humanity to experience pleasure within His guidelines. However, our human nature shifts our focus from what God has given us to what God has forbidden.

One day, I was lamenting to my friend BJ about another friendship that had recently ended. "I'm devastated. Lexi was such a good friend, and I don't know what went wrong. We always had the best time, and I miss her."

"Lisa, it's okay to grieve the loss," he replied. "But don't forget about the many other relationships you have been blessed with. I know you're sad, but don't take your other friends for granted. Invest your time in the friends that are here. You have more than you lost."

Likewise, you may have vices that you've used to pursue pleasure throughout your life. When you lean away from those routes to pleasure and lean into God's path, you will miss them. You will grieve. Friend, don't let your focus linger on the restricted pleasures. Instead, look for what God has provided. Call out everything He gave you to enjoy in Him, like your family, your home, your job, your friends, your church, good restaurants, traveling, nature, and so on. I recognize that some of these have been sources of pain for you and that others have been sources of joy. Focus on the joys. Take inventory of your life: Make a list of all the people, places, and things God has given you to enjoy so that, in moments when you are tempted to focus on the restrictions, you can see that more is available to you than is restricted from you.

God wants you to experience His love, which will bring you more happiness than anything else you could ever experience. God's way is the only path to pleasure that will ever bring you true fulfillment. None of the pleasures you choose will ever give you satisfaction. But when you completely surrender your pursuit of pleasure on your terms and pursue it on His terms, then you will experience true peace, joy, and abundant life.

IS GOD'S WAY WORTH IT?

When I started working out, my trainer told me not to look at the scale daily. He understood that if I monitored the scale as an indicator of progress, then I would be discouraged because I wouldn't lose pounds initially; I would lose inches. When you're sacrificing, you want to see results. You want to know that your diet and exercise are making a positive impact. The same is true when we sacrifice our way of pursuing pleasure for God's way. We're asking, *Is it worth it? Will it pay off?*

As a teenager, I decided that I would wait until marriage to have sex. It wasn't just a spiritual decision but also seemed wise and practical at the time. In my mind, it was the best way to avoid STDs, unwanted pregnancy, and severe heartbreak.

As I got older, I wondered if I had made the right decision. Was I denying myself pleasure? Was following God's way outdated? Was I getting the short end of the stick? At times, I really struggled. However, now, at thirty-seven, I'm thankful I decided to wait. I praise God I didn't have sex with gentlemen I dated. Not because they are all bad men but because the breakups were easier to navigate when I hadn't given them all of me. Imagine how much more difficult it would have been for me to navigate the devastating end of my relationship with Clark if sex had been involved. God's restriction was His protection.

Waiting doesn't guarantee that I will get married or that my marriage will be easy if I do. But waiting helps me keep a peaceful and sober mind. Waiting guards my heart and helps me avoid the unexpected potential side effects of premarital sex.

You may be experiencing sacrifices in another area of restricted pleasure. And perhaps you're having a hard time seeing what the sacrifice will produce. There may be moments when you feel like denying yourself has brought you more pain than blessing. Perhaps you waited until you got married to have sex, and your marriage still ended in divorce. Or maybe you were young and excited when you came to faith, and you stopped all worldly pleasures and pursuits to follow God. Now, years later, nothing in life has gone how you hoped it would, and you're wondering if any of the sacrifices ever mattered.

Friend, I get it. Looking over your life and not seeing any benefit from the sacrifices you made is discouraging. Can you imagine going to the gym every day for a year, eating healthy, and not losing a single pound? I would be devastated and feel like I wasted a year of sacrifice.

Perhaps you feel that way about your life. Perhaps you feel like you wasted your time and would have been happier following your way, not God's. Perhaps you've grown bitter toward God and now you want to give up.

It's okay to be there; it's human to be there. I've been there. But I want you to know your sacrifice isn't in vain. I hate working out, but I realized that I never regret working out. Anytime I leave the gym, I'm thankful I went. You may feel disappointed at times, but you will never regret your choice to sacrifice and pursue pleasure God's way. Let me explain.

Dr. K. Edward Copeland, lead pastor of New Zion

Baptist Church in Rockford, Illinois, once told me, "When this life is all said and done, God won't owe you anything." What he meant is that God will always honor and bless you for your sacrifice. His blessing may not happen in this life, but it will manifest itself in the next. If you're concerned only about seeing the reward in this life, you will always feel like God disappointed you.

When I worked at Bank of America and Merrill Lynch, I enrolled in the 401(k) retirement plan. Each pay period, my employers would match a percentage of the amount I put into the account from my paycheck. However, I knew the money in the 401(k) wasn't for now; it was for later. I could access the benefits of my sacrifice only once I retired.

Similarly, in our walk with the Lord, when we sacrifice for Him, we make deposits in our heavenly 401(k), and some of them we can access only once we retire from this earth. Jesus said, "Don't store up treasures here on earth, where moths eat them and rust destroys them, and where thieves break in and steal. Store your treasures in heaven, where moths and rust cannot destroy, and thieves do not break in and steal."[11]

When you understand that heaven is forever and earth is temporary, your perspective shifts. Your suffering and sacrifice without seeing reward is temporary. In heaven, God "will wipe every tear from [your] eyes, and there will be no more death or sorrow or crying or pain."[12] You will finally get to access your heavenly 401(k) and see the benefits you received for pursuing pleasure God's way and not your own. Your sacrifice and suffering are not in vain. God sees you, and He will reward you. In the end, "God won't owe you anything."

PRAYER

God,

Forgive me for pursuing pleasure on my terms. But if I'm honest, I resent You. Life has been challenging, and I pray for relief, but it seems like You don't hear me. So I picked up my own vices to help with the pain, but they have only created addictions that I can't seem to break free from. I feel like I'm caught in a cycle that brings me more pain. I don't know how to get out of this. I want to trust You, but I'm afraid You will let me down. I'm wondering, Do You even care? Do You love me? Do You have good intentions for me? Help me see Your love for me, the good You want for me, because I need Your help.

God, please help me see things the way You see them.

In Jesus's name, amen.

PURPOSE

Purpose has been so misunderstood and abused.

—DR. ANITA PHILLIPS,

in an interview with Oprah Winfrey

Lying across the sofa in the room she rented, Erica cradled her phone, flipping back and forth between Facebook and Instagram. With each scroll, there was a sting, a reminder that she was still not where she wanted to be. Every time her finger swiped up, she would see another grand life update: a friend reaching a milestone, a relative closing on a house, a childhood neighbor getting engaged, and a cousin announcing a new dream job.

Erica's face was calm, but her heart was erupting like a volcano. She couldn't contain it anymore. She finally blurted out, "What's my purpose?"

In college, she had so many hopes and aspirations. She dreamed of a life filled with purpose and passion. But here she was, feeling trapped in a job she hated. She had no loving partner to enjoy pillow talk with, no infant hands clutching her fingers, and no home that she could call her own. All she felt she had was the unrelenting pain of aimlessly walking through life.

Every Sunday, Erica led a Bible study group with a faith that seemed unshakable. But beneath the surface, doubt threatened to overtake her. She wrestled with her faith, questioning why her prayers for direction seemed to fall on deaf ears. "God, can You hear me?" she'd whisper as she lay in bed at night.

One evening, over the phone, Erica poured her heart out to me. She lamented, "I've read books and listened to podcasts, seeking answers, but I still don't know my purpose. God seems silent."

Like Erica, everyone is looking for purpose, but few know where to find it. Many think purpose is found in careers, families, romantic relationships, friendships, kids—the list goes on and on. Yet they are continually disappointed when no matter how much they search for meaning, they can't find it. Careers come up short. Relationships come up short. Families come up short. Even faith seems to come up short.

The commercialization of purpose in America has intensified the pain point. A new book, post, or podcast on purpose pops up every week. Yet when we can't seem to find it, depression and hopelessness set in.

Why is purpose so hard to find? Why do we come up empty-handed just when we think we've grasped it? If everyone has a purpose, why do so many seem unable to locate it?

In a recent television interview, I watched a political pundit rail against critical race theory (CRT)—a talking point in many political speeches and cultural arguments. He was adamant that critical race theory was one of the biggest dangers to our society. He was passionate and confident as he articulated the assumed dangers of CRT. However, when the host asked him to explain CRT, the pundit struggled. He couldn't come up with a clear definition of the theory he was attacking.

Watching that interview was painful. How was he so obsessed with tearing down something he didn't fully understand? Why devote that much energy to something you can barely define? While you may view the pundit with disbelief and disdain, if you look closely, you may see yourself. When it comes to purpose, are you, too, speaking about something you don't fully know how to define? How can you find it if you can't define it?

At the core, purpose signifies the very reason for our existence. For many individuals, their quest for purpose intensifies during times of hardship. They want to gain clarity amid the storm. They hope that by understanding their purpose—the reason for their existence—they will gain meaning in their suffering.

There must be more than pain; it must produce some good. Our minds echo Paul's words in Romans as we encounter painful realities: "We know that all things work together for good to them that love God, to them who are the called according to his purpose."[1]

We see how deeply connected purpose and suffering are when we look at the Cross. The Savior of the world, Jesus, experienced great suffering. He could endure because He knew the good it would produce: the world's salvation. His suffering created the bridge of reconciliation between God and humanity.

While ours isn't as weighty as His, we also have purpose in suffering: to be conformed to the image of God. That means our actions reflect the actions of Jesus. That means our responses reflect the Jesus we claim to serve. Purpose is about who we become and not what we achieve. The means God uses to get us to look more like Him is the journey of purpose.

Purpose is about who we become and not what we achieve.

When I set up a new Apple product, I'm always asked if I've read the terms and conditions. And I always check yes, even when I haven't. Have you ever done the same? Maybe it's not an Apple product; maybe it's Samsung or a new video game or app. Or perhaps you never read the instructions on how to set up that new piece of Ikea furniture or the bookshelf from Walmart. How could we possibly know what we're agreeing to if we don't read the terms and conditions? Or how do we even know we built that desk correctly if we don't read the instructions?

Friend, I wish terms and conditions were the only things we've agreed to that we haven't read, but unfortunately, for many, it's the Bible too. Many people have signed up to be Christians but never actually read the manual—the Bible—from cover to cover. So what they believe about God and His purpose for their lives ends up twisted. Their understanding of their godly purpose is shaped not by God's Word but by assumptions or woven-together pieces of Scripture that create a theology disconnected from the full context of the Bible. Or worse, by an Americanized view of purpose that centers around financial prosperity and celebrity. Without reading God's manual—His terms, conditions, and instructions—how we view everything will be distorted.

So before we go any further, let's distinguish between a biblical view of purpose and an Americanized view of purpose. For this chapter, let's reframe purpose to gain clarity on what our culture sees as purpose and what God says about it.

PURPOSE ISN'T A PLATFORM

I remember watching an interview with a movie star a few years ago. He told the interviewer that he was still trying to find his purpose. How could he not know his purpose? After all, he has a global audience. Aren't followers on your social media accounts and subscribers to your YouTube channel essential elements to having a purpose?

Unfortunately, many people think so. If it doesn't result in a platform, they assume it's not purposeful. However, this famous gentleman knew what you and I so often miss: A platform doesn't mean you are living out your purpose. An Americanized view of purpose may suggest that it does. But public affirmation doesn't mean you are walking in God's plan for your life.

Paul was a successful Pharisee. He had prestige and a platform. But he wasn't walking in his purpose—being conformed to the image of God. He persecuted Christians and lived outside God's will. However, when he accepted Jesus and submitted his life to Him, Paul was able to fulfill the purposes God had for him. He was persecuted, thrown in jail, and so much more. Yet he was conformed to the image of God and left a legacy that has influenced the lives of billions.

Consider your life. You may not have millions of followers on TikTok or national recognition. But those things don't determine your value or give your life meaning. Your purpose will never be found in worldly status. It can be found only in surrendering your life to the divine.

PURPOSE UNLIMITED

In undergrad, I started a successful Christian T-shirt line with a friend. Our business touched so many lives, and the shirts sparked conversations with unbelievers. My purpose in that moment was to reach both believers and unbelievers in Christ's name—to reflect His image in the darkness. In 2015, I turned the business over to my friend, and my purpose for that season of my life ended. But my purpose in life didn't end. Right now, God has me leading Jude 3 Project. But in twenty years, I could be doing something else. My purpose isn't limited to one thing. It's the sum of my obedience to God in every season, because there is purpose in every place.

You don't have to limit your purpose to a particular career, season, platform, service activity, or achievement. If you did, then there would be no reason for you to live after that moment, achievement, or season was past. If your sole goal in life was to accomplish one thing and you completed it at age twenty, what would you do with the rest of your life?

Friend, God has different purposes for you in every space you occupy. So instead of thinking about purpose as an abstract idea that can't be explained or obtained, think of purpose as obedience to God wherever He places you. Then purpose becomes reachable, lifelong, and easier to walk in.

PURPOSE ISN'T ESCAPE

Last year, when I started working out with a trainer, I hated to hear the alarm go off at five in the morning. I would roll over and hit snooze twice before finally getting up. When I got to the gym, I had to start each workout with fifteen minutes of cardio on the treadmill. That was the easiest part. Then we would move to weights. My trainer would always remind me that it was not just about lifting weights but also about lifting them properly. The weights would be heavy however I lifted them, but only when I lifted them the proper way would I see the desired results.

The same principle is true in life: Whether we live out our purpose or not, life will be challenging. Knowing the purpose of the load can make it more bearable, but it doesn't mean the load won't be heavy. Recognizing this reality helps us endure difficulties "as a good soldier."[2]

I remember waking up the week COVID-19 shut the world down, hoping that it was a dream. I was afraid and in shock, and I couldn't fully process what was happening. Just when I thought I was getting my mind around it, my grandfather passed away. I was heartbroken.

While I was getting dressed for his funeral, I got the text that my mentor had died. My knees buckled. I fell on my bed and wept. It all felt like too much. The pain was gut-wrenching. To make matters worse, I had to navigate funerals with pandemic restrictions and precautions. Grief is already difficult, but it's compounded when you can't hug the ones you love because of social distancing or see their faces because of masks. The whole year was painful. At the same time, Jude 3 Project was experiencing tremendous growth. I had to hold purpose, pain, and progress in tension. While I was getting the desired results from my purpose, I wasn't exempt from the harsh realities of life.

Have you ever experienced that? Have you ever had to hold joy and pain together? Have you had to navigate the death of a parent at the same time as a job promotion? Or graduation from college along with a broken heart? Or maybe it was the loss of a job and the birth of a child? Life is bitter and sweet, and often purpose lives in the tension between them.

PURPOSE BEYOND YOUR LIFETIME

On the eve of his assassination, Dr. Martin Luther King, Jr., gave one of his most powerful speeches to a packed crowd in Memphis. He prophetically declared, "We've got some difficult days ahead. . . . I've seen the Promised Land. I may not get there with you. But I want you to know tonight, that we, as a people, will get to the Promised Land."[3] The good that came from Dr. King's work and suffering wasn't realized in his lifetime. He didn't see all the benefits of his purpose. Still, many generations are experiencing the benefits now because Dr. King lived out of his purpose then.

You may never experience the full benefits of your purpose, but the journey God has for you isn't just for you. The road you are on to be more like Him and the rewards you will receive are also for those who will come after you.

PURPOSE BEYOND GIFTS

Our gifts are our strengths, and it's natural to think that God's purpose for us can be found in knowing what we do best. However, God isn't interested only in using our strengths; He also wants to use our weaknesses to glorify Himself. This means that part of our purpose is tied not just to our gifts but to our weaknesses.

I'm not too fond of confrontation. The thought of it used to give me anxiety. I don't like conflict, and I want everyone to get along. But part of the platform God has graced me with is a national conference called Courageous Conversations, the pillar event in the Jude 3 Project brand. This conference brings together the leading scholars, pastors, and other thought leaders from conservative and progressive spaces in the Black community to have hard conversations about church and culture. At Courageous Conversations, there are four panelists—all with differing views—and a moderator per panel. Thankfully, the conversations are always civil.

In addition to hosting the conference, I've been on a couple of panels. I always have to talk myself into it. I really don't enjoy moderating and debating against someone with different views from me, especially in front of a crowd of people. Why would God pick me to lead an event like this? Because He is faithful to His word.

When the apostle Paul prayed three times about a thorn in his flesh, the Lord responded, "My grace is sufficient for you, for my power is made perfect in weakness."[4] Like with Paul, God used my weakness to show off His strength. After one of the conferences, some clips of me speaking went viral. I received many messages from people telling me how they were blessed by what I said. They saw God, not me.

Have you noticed in your own life that God has used the things you don't like to make you more like Him? God's purpose has shone through your weakness for His glory.

PURPOSE AND PAIN

Suffering intensifies our pursuit of purpose. We want to find meaning in our suffering because we hope that dis-

covering our purpose will alleviate the pain. But knowing the why doesn't always help with the pain.

Suppose a drunk driver hits and kills your family mem-
ber. Do you think that an autopsy would alleviate your
pain? An autopsy may help you understand how the impact of the drunk driver's car ended your loved one's life,
but it does nothing to curb the grief. Perhaps you even
hear from the driver that he had lost his job and was dis-
traught because he could no longer care for his family, so
he turned to alcohol as a balm to his heart. While that
could help you understand why the driver was drunk, it
can't bring back the one you lost and does little to nothing to lessen your suffering.

Friend, if you aren't careful, pain can become all-
encompassing, blurring your purpose. When pain is at
the helm, your broken heart can damage your senses and
alter your ability to discern the voice and direction of
God, the only One capable of revealing your purpose, the
reason for your life on earth.

Your creator knows you inside and out. He wove you
together in your mother's womb. He knows the intimate
parts of your heart. Only He can reveal why He created
you. Only He can tell you your reason for living. Without
God, you are walking through life with noise-canceling
headphones and a blindfold. To hear and see Him—to
know your purpose—you must remove the headphones
and blindfold of pain. You must pursue healing.

HEALING, THEN PURPOSE

I know a woman named Danielle. She has a charismatic presence, even though she experienced horrific childhood trauma. Against all odds, she seems able to function at a high level, and year after year, she is on a new God-ordained mission. At first glance, her passionate pursuits seem commendable. She dives headfirst into every new endeavor with her diverse talents and garners impressive traction. Yet before she can complete her mission, something always goes wrong. She seems magnetically drawn to some conflict that pushes her to quit. The flames of the opportunity are snuffed out as quickly as they ignited.

If you look closely, you can see that instead of confronting her past and healing, Danielle chose to pursue achievement and impact as her reason for being, hoping that, with purpose in her grasp, she would mend her broken heart and fractured soul. However, they were a poor substitute for God's healing and were never able to penetrate the trauma. Danielle entered therapy to help her understand her past. Yet even with knowledge about her pain, she hasn't implemented the strategies her therapist gave her to confront it. She still has her blindfold and headphones on.

Despite her internal turmoil, doors keep opening for Danielle. To her, these open doors are God's divine direction, so she enters them boldly. But her understanding of

God's direction is hindered by unaddressed trauma, and she continues to aimlessly chase influence to find meaning.

Danielle's struggle is common and easy for all of us to fall prey to. Why? Because tackling a task is easier than facing trauma. But how can we ever fix what we refuse to face?

Suppose a person has lung cancer; the doctor explains that they got it from smoking. He helped identify the source of the problem, but that does nothing to alleviate the pain the patient is experiencing. If the doctor stopped at the explanation without developing a treatment plan, we would see him as incompetent. Telling the patient why they have cancer doesn't mean much if you don't have a way to treat it.

Similarly, God doesn't just want us to be able to explain why we are hurt. He has developed a treatment plan through Jesus to heal damaged parts of us. When we are whole and healed, we can hear God clearly. So how do we heal? I believe there are four steps to healing.

1. Be in Right Relationship with God

The starting point of our healing journey is a right relationship with God, which comes only through repenting of our sins and accepting Jesus as our Lord and Savior.

2. Confess Your Sins in Community

I firmly believe in James 5:16: "Confess your faults one to another, and pray one for another, that ye may be healed"

(KJV). My dad put it this way: "Confession to God brings forgiveness of sin, but confession to man brings healing from sin." Your healing isn't just a by-product of prayer and repentance. God has rigged your life for community. You won't obtain healing without sharing your struggles, failures, and traumas with others. When you share your hurts with others and pray with them, healing comes.

You may be thinking, *I can't trust people in the church.* Christians may be the source of your pain. I get it. I understand. However, the place that hurt you is the same place God wants to heal you. If church is too hard for you to visit right now, you can begin to act out the principle of confession with a therapist. To be healed, you must talk to someone. Healing will never be a result of isolation; it's a product of community.

3. Forgive

I've often heard, "Unforgiveness is like drinking poison and waiting on the other person to die." Unforgiveness intensifies the pain of the trauma and creates more damage as time goes on. This seems to echo the writer of Hebrews: "See to it that no one fails to obtain the grace of God; that no 'root of bitterness' springs up and causes trouble, and by it many become defiled."[5] Bitterness is a by-product of unforgiveness, and if you don't forgive, bitterness will contaminate your relationship with God, yourself, and others. The only way to be free from the rot and pain of the wound is to forgive.

4. Repair

My devotional life took a significant hit during the pandemic. I was burdened by grief and busyness. I was grieving the deaths of my grandfather and my mentor and trying to manage the success of Jude 3 Project. My soul felt disconnected from my body. I was watching my life happen, but I felt like I wasn't a part of it.

My friend Watson recommended that I get an app called Centering Prayer to help structure my devotional life. One day, during my thirty minutes of silence and meditation, I heard the Lord say clearly, "Go make it right with them." And He didn't leave me wondering who "them" was! He gave me a list of people. Some of them I had wronged, and others had wronged me. Do you know how humbling it was to call people out of the blue, discuss old issues, and apologize? With each conversation, I felt lighter, more whole. I didn't realize how much I had been carrying. The freedom and healing I needed were tied to the work of repair.

Repairing isn't just for me; it's for you too. Go do the work of repair. Jesus charges us with this work in the Gospels: "If you are presenting a sacrifice at the altar in the Temple and you suddenly remember that someone has something against you, leave your sacrifice there at the altar. Go and be reconciled to that person. Then come and offer your sacrifice to God."[6]

However, Jesus didn't stop there. Later in Matthew, He gave further instruction: "If another believer sins against you, go privately and point out the offense. If the other person listens and confesses it, you have won that person back."[7]

Jesus doesn't let us off the hook. Whether we have hurt someone or they have hurt us, we are required to initiate the work of repair.

As you walk through the healing steps, you'll no longer be aimlessly feeling around for your purpose. Instead, your blindfold will fall from your eyes, and you will see God's path. Your headphones will tumble to the ground, and you'll hear His voice saying, "This way, My child." The burden of finding your purpose will lift from your shoulders as you trust God to guide you.

OBEY GOD AND FIND PURPOSE

I never wanted to be an apologist. My plan was to go to New York City and work on Wall Street. But during college, I felt God leading me to take a New Testament class at the University of North Florida, and my whole life changed.

On the first day of the course, my professor declared,

"I'm going to change everything you thought you knew about Jesus."

Ha. I'm a pastor's kid. What could be so hard about a New Testament class? My parents taught me the Bible, and I've been to Sunday school. I know the ropes. This will be easy.

Turns out, New Testament at a university was very different from Sunday school, especially when our textbook was written by a New Testament scholar who doesn't believe the Bible was divinely inspired. Dr. Bart Ehrman's view was a stark contrast to what I had heard at my childhood church. I knew God had led me to take this class, but my faith was crumbling. I didn't know what to believe.

When my father saw me struggling, he introduced me to apologetics—the defense of my faith through logic and embodying the message of the gospel. Apologetics was water to my thirsty soul. By understanding the history of and basis for my core beliefs, I learned how to navigate the class, argue for my faith, and persevere. I fell in love with apologetics.

Throughout my studies, I didn't see many people in apologetics that looked like me. Most of the prominent apologists were older white men. *Someone should do something about that,* I thought. I didn't realize it at the time, but God was preparing me for part of my purpose: founding and running Jude 3 Project.

I wrestled with my faith during that class, and now I can emotionally connect with others who are in their own deconstruction process. They are willing to confide in me and listen because I've felt the pain and confusion as well. When I jumped headfirst into apologetics, I learned how to defend my faith, and now I offer experience and guidance to others on their journey to reconstruction. *I* didn't have to make sense out of the struggle. I only had to obey God and trust Him to reveal my purpose. *God* made sense out of my wrestling. He revealed the fruit of my suffering.

My friend Erica learned to obey God to find her purpose as well. After podcasts and books didn't help, she began to study biblical characters' lives to find solutions. She noticed that no biblical characters she looked at were obsessed with their purpose. They just providentially stepped into it when they walked in obedience to God. Erica started to question her view of purpose and shifted to lean into God's view of purpose. Once she reframed her understanding of purpose, Erica didn't obsess over what her purpose was. She knew God would reveal it over time. Instead, she focused on simple acts of obedience to Him daily. She unburdened herself from the pressure of finding her purpose.

Friend, the key to finding your purpose is to obey God. If you walk faithfully with Him and obey Him daily in the little things, then you, too, will look back and realize you are living out the purpose God has called you to. You don't have to look for it. Purpose will find you.

PURPOSE HAS MANY FORMS

In the American commercialization of purpose, we seek to put our name in lights. We want a purpose that will get us one million followers on Instagram, but that isn't what God promises. God's purpose for us is to become like Jesus and reflect Him in every space we occupy.

My grandfather Louis Fields, Sr., was the sharpest man you could ever meet. He was kind, funny, and hardworking. He was a loving husband, father, and grandfather. He never had his name in lights, but he loved and cared for his family. To him, purpose was about being a good man. He wasn't looking for anything fancy; he just wanted to follow Christ and be a good man for his family and community.

God has a purpose for you in your family, at your job, at your church, and in any other space you occupy. But if you achieve great things in life and don't love your family and friends well, you have missed your purpose. If you are a hero to the world but a failure at home, you have missed your purpose. If your faith is on public display but has produced no private transformation, you have missed your purpose. Because like my grandfather knew, purpose is not about what you achieve but rather about who you become.

When you reflect Jesus to the world through your everyday life, you walk in purpose. When you glorify God

through your life, you walk in purpose. Purpose isn't complex; you don't have to endure unnecessary pressure from
society's view of purpose. You don't have to keep playing
hide-and-seek to find it. Be faithful to God wherever you
are, walk in obedience to Him, and your purpose will take
many forms.

PRAYER

God,

My life seems meaningless right now. It hasn't turned out the way I thought it would, and I'm disappointed. There has to be more to life than what I'm experiencing right now. I know I'm called to reflect Jesus in the world, but I'm still trying to make sense of what that means for me. I want to see and hear You clearly, but my unhealed heart makes knowing You difficult.

God, I want desperately to be in right relationship with You so my healing journey can begin. Give me the courage to enter Christian community again so I can confess my faults to others and receive the healing I desire. Give me a heart that is open to forgiving those who hurt me. I don't want to let bitterness continue to ruin my life. Grant me the boldness to do the work of repair in relationships where I have been wronged or have done wrong.

I need You to guide me and help me understand purpose from Your perspective. I need You, God. Please help.

In Jesus's name, amen.

PROTECTION

The LORD is my rock, my fortress, and my savior;
>   my God is my rock, in whom I find protection.
He is my shield, the power that saves me,
>   and my place of safety.

—David, Psalm 18:2

On the eve of an apologetics conference, speakers from various regions gathered in a tiny Atlanta restaurant. I soon found myself engaged in conversation with a speaker from Nigeria. I asked, "What are the apologetics challenges you face back in Nigeria?"

He paused for a moment and then said, "Syncretism."

I asked him to elaborate.

He leaned in. "Many in Nigeria embraced Christianity, leaving behind ancestral African religions. But over time, they continued to face the harsh realities of terrorism they thought God would protect them from. So they begin to add African spirituality back into their religious practices. They hope it will provide an extra shield, because they have begun to doubt if the God of Christianity alone is sufficient."

The gravity of his words pushed me into deep reflection. We may live in different places, but our struggles aren't that different. Many Americans are wondering if the God of the Bible is enough to protect them.

God's protection is in question when we think about the atrocities in our world: school shootings, sexual violence, systemic injustice, slavery. Where is His protection for the victims of those evils? Can we trust God if we aren't sure He has protected us or will protect us in those scenarios?

These questions create real pain for us. How do we navigate these problematic realities? What truths about God can we hold on to even when we don't understand His ways?

MAKE IT MAKE SENSE

As we try to make sense of the suffering that God allows, one of the first things to remember is that God's ways aren't like ours. Philosopher Dr. Vince Vitale, who has co-authored a book on suffering, gave a brilliant illustration demonstrating the gap between our ways and God's: "When I take my dog, Buster, to the vet and Buster has to experience a painful needle, Buster doesn't understand why that's the case. And if I sit Buster down on the couch and I try to explain to him that this is important so you don't get some terrible disease, I don't get very far." He continued, "That's not because of some lack of ability on my part. It's not that I'm not a good enough communicator. Buster simply isn't the sort of being who can understand why I do some of the things that I do."[1] When two different beings are in communication, comprehension is limited. If God sat us down and explained His ways, we wouldn't fully understand them, because we aren't the same kind of being. We are human; God is divine.

As I was growing up, when our family ate out, my parents would ask my brothers and me where we wanted to eat. I might say McDonald's, one of my brothers might say Burger King, and my other brother might say Taco Bell. There was never a consensus. Ultimately, my parents would have to pick what they wanted, because we couldn't agree.

When we think about what God allows, consider what would happen if He asked every person on the planet who has ever existed what He should do about suffering. Like with my and my siblings' dinner choices, there would be no consensus. Since that is the case, He has to do what is best based on what He knows about the past, present, and future. He can't consult with humans. He has to consult with Himself. Paul said that God "works all things according to the counsel of His will."[2]

Ryan Gilliam, a successful business owner, has been my business mentor for almost ten years. I rarely make a business decision without calling Ryan first. His experience makes him qualified for me to consult with. While I have great friends around me, they don't help me in matters of business. It isn't that I don't love them or value their insight; I don't consult them because they don't have Ryan's experience.

God doesn't have a Ryan. No one has ever existed like Him. No one has experience creating a world but Him. No one has all power but Him. No one knows the past, present, and future but Him. So He can't consult with anyone but Himself. Job found this out when he questioned God about the great suffering he was enduring.

Job was an upright man in the Bible who suffered the loss of his wealth, children, and health in a series of traumatic events. Understandably, he was frustrated with the suffering he endured, because he felt like he had been punished unfairly. He asked God to explain Himself. God reminded Job that he didn't have the experience for this kind of consultation:

> Where were you when I laid the foundations of the earth?
>   Tell me, if you know so much.
> Who determined its dimensions
>   and stretched out the surveying line?
> What supports its foundations,
>   and who laid its cornerstone

as the morning stars sang together
  and all the angels shouted for joy?

Who kept the sea inside its boundaries
  as it burst from the womb,
and as I clothed it with clouds
  and wrapped it in thick darkness?
For I locked it behind barred gates,
  limiting its shores.
I said, "This far and no farther will you come.
  Here your proud waves must stop!"

Have you ever commanded the morning to appear
  and caused the dawn to rise in the east?
Have you made daylight spread to the ends of the earth,
  to bring an end to the night's wickedness?[3]

When you don't have the same experience, someone's choices might not make sense to you. I've made several business decisions that my friends didn't understand. God's ways may never make sense to you, but you can still trust Him. Job never found out why God allowed him to suffer. However, he continued to trust God because he understood that God knew more than him and had more experience than him.

Dr. Timothy Keller noted, "Just because we don't see a reason why God allows evil and suffering doesn't mean there isn't one."[4] This realization pushes us to trust in

God's character. If you believe that God is good, just, loving, and faithful, then when you experience suffering, you must choose to trust Him instead of abandoning Him.

FREE WILL LIMITED

When God created humanity, He decided, based on the counsel of His own will, to give us free will. He said, "Let us make man in our image, after our likeness."[5] That means that we carry some of God's attributes. One of them is ultimate free will, known as His sovereignty. God does what He wants when He wants and how He wants. Therefore, if He created humanity in His image and likeness with limited amounts of His attributes, then He gifted us a limited amount of free will. We don't decide a lot about our lives: Where we are born, what family we are born into, our ethnicity, and our socioeconomic status are all predetermined for us. But God has given us free will in small doses.

We have a God-given right to choose. However, this right is a double-edged sword. One person's decision can affect another person positively or negatively. When Adam and Eve ate the fruit, they had no idea the Pandora's box they were opening for themselves and all humanity. They just did what they desired, what pleased them in the moment; they didn't know the consequences that would follow.

God gives us the freedom to choose, but we choose without knowing the effects that will follow. God is the only being that doesn't need guidance on decisions, because He has all knowledge and wisdom. We, however, are human beings with limited understanding, so we need someone without our limitations to guide us.

When we don't consult with God to help us make our decisions, we usually end up with negative consequences that cause us—and others—pain and suffering. God made us to be interdependent, so everything we do or say will have an impact on others. Our decisions have a domino effect. Ever since Adam and Eve ate the fruit from the tree, the dominoes have been falling.

When we try to make sense of the pain point of protection, we have to reckon with the negative impacts of free will, even when free will is limited. If God stripped free will from us, He would take part of His image from us. And without His image, who would we be? His image gives us our value because it's the very thing that makes us unique.

Dr. Dharius Daniels said, "There is a backside to every blessing."[6] The "backside" is the part of the blessing that we won't like. One of my favorite songs of all time is by the Notorious B.I.G., featuring Puff Daddy and Mase, called "Mo Money Mo Problems." Part of the song's chorus says, "It's like the more money we come across, the more problems we see."[7] What they were sharing in the music is the same thing Dr. Daniels explained: Blessings come with their own burdens.

Such is the case with free will; it's a blessing because it reminds us that humanity was made in God's image, but it's a burden because a consequence of free will is the reality of evil. A person can choose good or evil, to obey God or disobey. In the words of Job, "Shall we indeed accept good from God, and shall we not accept adversity?"[8] Free will has a sweet and a bitter side; if we celebrate the sweet part, we must also embrace the bitter. Maturity demands that we hold them in tension.

GOD MADE IT GOOD

Joseph's story is one of the most fascinating stories in the Bible. His brothers were jealous of the love their father had for him, so they faked Joseph's death and sold him into slavery. While enslaved, he was falsely accused of rape by his master's wife and imprisoned. He experienced great suffering at the hands of multiple people. As you read the story, you may think, *This isn't fair! Where is God? How could He let this happen to a faithful man like Joseph?* I'm sure Joseph had the same questions. However, at the end of the story, we find out that God was using all this hardship to save Joseph's family.

God knew that a famine was coming and Joseph's family wasn't going to have food, so He allowed all these things to happen to Joseph to position him to interpret Pharaoh's dreams, which led him to be the second-in-command in all of Egypt. When Joseph's brothers asked him for forgiveness, he responded, "You intended to harm me, but God intended it for good to accomplish what is now being done, the saving of many lives."[9]

God can take the broken pieces of evil decisions and create good for His people. Scripture is filled with stories of Him working behind the scenes. Look closely at the genealogy of Jesus in the first chapter of Matthew. Do you see all the wrong choices that filled the lives of people in His lineage? God picked up the pieces and brought salvation through them. He doesn't commit evil, but He can work through it to create good for those who love Him, even if we don't see His hand right away.

God can take the broken pieces of evil decisions and create good.

Jesus received word that His dear friend Lazarus was ill. Instead of going to see Lazarus immediately, He delayed. When He finally arrived, Lazarus had already been dead for four days. Lazarus's sisters, Martha and Mary, blamed Jesus. They both said that if He had come earlier, their brother wouldn't have died.[10]

Have you ever felt that way? Have you ever felt that if Jesus had come when you prayed, you wouldn't have had to suffer? Have you ever blamed Him for your pain?

Maybe you're going through a harsh reality right now. You may not *feel* God's protection. But take heart: "In all things God works for the good of those who love him, who have been called according to his purpose."[11]

Jesus's delay wasn't denial or indifference. He raised Lazarus, and many people believed. Joseph endured many trials, but God positioned him to rescue His people. Like He did with Lazarus and Joseph, God will use the suffering you experience to help others believe. He will bring beauty from ashes, life from death, joy from pain, and peace from chaos. Friend, none of your pain and suffering will be wasted. God will recycle it.

SUFFERING SAVIOR

When I was young, our church was renovated. My parents worked alongside the church members: moving materials, remodeling, and cleaning up. They never required the members to do something they themselves weren't willing to do. I admired them. They modeled what it looks like for a leader to demonstrate what the leader demands.

Their leadership style wasn't new; Jesus demonstrated servant leadership more than two thousand years ago on the cross. He knew humanity would have to suffer because of sin, so He allowed Himself to suffer. Jesus doesn't require us to experience what He hasn't already experienced. He has suffered too. He knows what it feels like to grieve someone you love; remember, He wept at the death of Lazarus. He knows what it feels like to have a father not show up when you need him the most; remember, He cried out to God on the cross, "Why have you forsaken me?"[12] He knows what it's like to be falsely accused; that's how He got on the cross. He knows what it's like to have those close to you betray and deny their relationship with you; Judas betrayed Him, and Peter denied Him. He knows how it feels when the people you did the most for are ungrateful; that's been His consistent experience with humanity throughout history.

Jesus deeply sympathizes and empathizes with your lived experiences. He isn't a distant deity, untouched by pain and trauma. He intimately knows suffering. He has walked through it Himself. We can draw strength and hope from the fact that He understands. God chose not to exempt Himself from life's complexities so that He can showcase His immense love and commitment to us. God didn't bend the rules of free will for Himself. Instead, He allowed Himself to experience suffering and pain for the salvation of His people. He is so committed to being in right relationship with us, because of His great love for us, that He wouldn't circumvent His own process. He could have changed the rules for Himself, but He knew we needed a savior that could identify with us in order to intercede for us.

PROTECTION REVISITED

So why didn't God stop the terrorists from killing Christians in Nigeria? Why doesn't He protect children from being murdered? Why doesn't He stop shootings at schools? I don't have an emotionally satisfying answer that will make these evils any more palatable. Even knowing all I've outlined in this chapter, I still wrestle with what God allows. We may never know the answer, but we can trust that God does. We may never fully understand His ways, but we know that He is good, wise, and loving. We know that He will make everything right and good in His perfect time. And in our suffering, in our lack of protection, we can hold on to the truth: God is with us. He will never leave us or abandon us. Even death can't separate us from Him.

PRAYER

God,

Even after reading this chapter, I'm still wrestling with what You allow. I don't understand why You didn't protect me from the traumas I've experienced. I'm angry with You. I have so many questions. I understand free will. I know You suffered too. But navigating this pain is still difficult. I understand that You will work the suffering for my good, but I struggle to see how You will do that, because of all the pain I'm in.

I don't know how to reconcile these truths with my reality, but I know You can help me process the deep wounds in my soul. Help me trust Your character when difficult situations make me want to question You. God, I ask You to help me as I wrestle through this. Please help me see Your hand in the pain.

In Jesus's name, amen.

POWER

Power without love ends up being abuse.

—PASTOR LOUIS FIELDS, JR.

Daniel's father was a pastor, so he grew up in church, and he devoted his life to God at a young age. He was an honor roll student, a leader on his football team, and a faithful servant in his youth group. The school of his dreams offered him a football scholarship his senior year, and he accepted. Daniel was so excited he could hardly contain himself. Everything was coming together. All his prayers seemed to be answered.

The summer before college, Daniel went on a mission trip. However, shortly after arriving on the mission field, he had a tragic accident that changed his life. The accident caused an injury that stole his ability to play football. Daniel was devastated. He wrestled with questions like,

How could following God lead to such a huge disappointment? Where was God? Was He responsible for this? He doubted whether he could trust God with his life. Daniel was filled with pain, anger, and despair and made the difficult decision to leave the Christian faith and take matters into his own hands.

Daniel isn't alone in questioning God. If we're honest, we've all been there. Giving someone power over us, especially if we don't trust their decision-making skills, is difficult. Do you find yourself in this dilemma? You want to give God control, but you remember the pain you experienced when you gave Him control in a previous season. So you've taken the wheel. You want to be the captain of your own ship so you can steer your life away from pain. When we feel powerless, we find tools that will give us control and help us curate the life we want to live.

One spiritual practice that has become popular recently is healing crystals. Sonali Saujani, a crystal master healer, described crystals as energy-holding minerals that facilitate energy exchange with humans. Some people use crystals to control their surroundings and lives. For example, obsidian is thought to be able to protect people from negativity, remove emotional blockages, and foster strength, clarity, compassion, and self-discovery.[1]

Another widely adopted spiritual practice aimed at enhancing control is the burning of sage:

For healers and laypeople in traditional cultures, burning sage is used to achieve a healing state—or to solve or reflect upon spiritual dilemmas. . . .

Burning sage may also be used as a ritual tool to rid yourself—or your space—of negativity. This includes past traumas, bad experiences, or negative energies from others.[2]

Manifestation is another spiritual practice some people use to gain power over their lives. While there are different approaches, manifestation is rooted in the idea that your beliefs can create the life you want. For example, if you have enough belief that the universe will give you a spouse, career, house, car, and so on, then your desire will become reality.

These spiritual practices are attractive because they promise to help us take our power back—power over our surroundings, relationships, and future. We use crystals, sage, or manifestation to feel a modicum of power.

The truth is, though, you won't have complete control of your life. You can't control when you meet your spouse. You can't control whether or not you experience serious illness. You can't control what happens to your children. You can't control when your loved ones leave this world. You aren't in control; God is. To think otherwise is just an illusion.

When my nephew, LJ, was one year old, my mom

would watch him during the day, and sometimes they would visit my grandma's house. Whenever LJ was ready to leave, he would signal to my mom by walking toward my grandma's door. Now, while he may have decided it was time to go, he could do so only when my mom decided to leave. No matter how many times he walked toward the door, he had no control over what time they left. At that stage in his life, everything was determined for him: where he lived, what he wore, what he ate, and where he went.

While we may think that's just LJ's plight, this is our plight as well. We don't have complete control over our lives. As the writer of Proverbs stated, "We can make our plans, but the LORD determines our steps."[3]

Why does God determine our steps? Why does He get the control? Because He can pay the price.

THE PRICE OF POWER

As I was preparing for my first year of college, I decided I wanted to live in an off-campus apartment instead of a dorm. I convinced my parents to go with me to take a tour of the apartment complex. I was excited as we toured and checked out all the amenities. When we got in the car, my parents told me I was staying in the dorm. In typical teenage fashion, I got an attitude and told them I was an adult now and could choose where I wanted to stay. They responded with a simple question: "How will you pay for it?" At that moment, I knew I was staying in the dorm. Since they were the ones paying, they made the decision. I couldn't afford control; it cost too much.

Control is expensive. In the Carters' song "Boss," Jay-Z rapped, "Everybody's bosses till it's time to pay for the office, till them invoices separate the men from the boys."[4] Jay-Z was communicating that a boss is a boss only when they pay the cost. The price of being the boss of your life is too high for you to afford.

Only one person could afford the position. Jesus paid the cost on the cross to be the boss more than two thousand years ago when they hung Him high and stretched Him wide. He was crucified for our sins. His payment gave Him "all authority in heaven and on earth."[5]

Since the beginning, we've been looking for something that will give us power like Jesus's. Adam and Eve were the first to fall prey to this desire when they ate the fruit in an attempt to be God. However, any control we think we have is just a figment of our imagination, because we weren't made to be in control. God designed us to be led by Him.

When I moved to Lynchburg, Virginia, for seminary, I was unprepared for snow. I was born and raised in Florida and had never lived through a winter with snow. One night while I was sleeping, snow began to fall. When I woke up, my car was covered. I got ready for class and went outside, hoping to use my windshield wipers to clear it off. That was a bad idea; the snow was stuck. I didn't have an ice scraper or a snow brush, so I improvised with a CD case. Imagine this Florida girl outside, trying to scrape snow off her car with a CD case. It was a sight to see. I spent almost thirty minutes hacking away at the snow. By the time I finished, my CD case was broken because I had used it for something it wasn't designed for.

Like my CD case wasn't designed to be an ice scraper, you weren't designed to have full power over your life. The prophet Jeremiah stated, "I know, LORD, that our lives are not our own. We are not able to plan our own course."[6]

When you operate outside your design, you damage yourself. Instead, God asks us to give up control.

Does giving up control seem unsettling to you? Do you twitch at the thought of handing over the decision-making to someone else? What would happen if you flipped the script? Instead of feeling unsettled, what if you found comfort in relinquishing control?

My first assistant, Angela, was one of the most efficient assistants I've ever seen. She had corporate managerial experience, an MBA, and a mind geared toward the work. When we started planning for Jude 3 Project's national conference, I put everything in her hands because administrative tasks aren't my strength but Angela had the experience and knowledge. Letting her run it was wise. Could I have done a decent job? Sure. But Angela did an *excellent* job. I could rest easy, knowing the administrative tasks for the conference were in her hands.

God has more experience and knowledge, so letting Him take the lead is wiser than leading yourself. When He is in control, you can trust Him to make the best decisions for your life. Better yet, take comfort in His control, friend, because God's love and goodness make His power incorruptible.

POWER WITHOUT LOVE CORRUPTS

While God has all power, He has given humans limited power. In Genesis, He gave Adam power to name the animals. In Exodus, He gave Moses power to lead Israel. In Judges, He gave Deborah power over Israel as a judge.

Even today, God has given you power. You may feel powerless because of the pain you've experienced, but God has made you to be powerful. Before Jesus departed from this earth, He told His disciples that the Holy Spirit—the third person in the Trinity—would come in His place so that they would receive power: power over sin, power over the Enemy, and power to preach the gospel.[7] The same Holy Spirit lives in you today, making His power available to you as well. God gives us limited power that is subject to His authority.

When I worked for Bank of America, the CEO, Brian Moynihan, had power over all of Bank of America. However, under Brian were C-suite executives, presidents, vice chairs, managers, and supervisors. While Brian controlled all of Bank of America, some under him had been given limited control over specific aspects of the business. While they had some power, they were still under Brian's authority. In a similar way, when we think about the power God has given us, we must remember that we have some power but that it's still subject to God's authority.

Even though the power that we have is limited, it still must be stewarded with love. Without love in the mix, limited power becomes corrupt and causes harm. As our various traumas can attest, most of us know what it feels like to be on the receiving end of the corruption of power (sexual harassment, child abuse, or police brutality). When we've been hurt by someone with control over our lives, we seek power to prevent further harm from happening to us. But no amount of power can prevent damage. Those who have power in this world still experience suffering.

As I write this, President Joe Biden is the most powerful man in the United States. However, throughout his life, he has experienced one tragedy after another. In 1972, his first wife, Neilia, and their one-year-old daughter, Naomi, were killed in a car crash.[8] While he was a senator in 1988, Biden suffered from two brain aneurysms.[9] In 2015, his older son, Beau, died of brain cancer.[10] His younger son, Hunter, had a history of drug abuse.[11] Joe Biden is a powerful man, but he hasn't been exempt from life's hardships. The same can be said of powerful people across the globe—power will never be able to quell grief, trauma, and pain. Pain will still come; power isn't an escape.

Instead, we need to process and heal from the traumas we experience. If we don't, then we can subconsciously hurt others. As the common phrase goes, "Hurt people hurt people." But creating pain by trying to escape pain will only create a generational cycle of trauma. To stop the cycle, we must steward the power God has given us well. And to steward our power well, we need to be on guard against the three ways power can become corrupted in us.

First, power can be corrupted by fear. If your desire for complete control is due to your unprocessed trauma, then your passion for power is rooted in fear, not love. The Bible says that fear torments.[12] Fear eats away at your soul, creates paranoia, and blinds you to reality. When this happens, you are often unaware of the damage you may do to others. Adding power to that is a recipe for disaster.

Second, power can be corrupted when deception is used to gain or maintain control. Slave owners would twist the Bible to stay in control and manipulate enslaved people into submission. There is no greater evidence of this than the Slave Bible. The Slave Bible was a highly redacted version of the Bible that didn't include passages about liberation and equality.[13] Dr. Anthony Schmidt of the Museum of the Bible noted, "About 90 percent of the Old Testament is missing [and] 50 percent of the New Testament is missing."[14] While the reality of a distorted version of the Bible is sickening, it's also instructive. When I encounter Black students who struggle with whether or not Christianity is for them, I remind them of the perversion of the Bible—how slave owners didn't want our people to read the whole Bible—and that reading all sixty-six books from cover to cover is a protest against white supremacy. Because knowing the whole truth is the only way to overcome a lie.

Finally, the power you have will be corrupted when love isn't involved, specifically if you don't love God, yourself, and people well. Let's start with the primary piece of this equation—loving God—because you can't love yourself and others until you learn how to love God.

One of the most popular relationship books of all time is Dr. Gary Chapman's *The 5 Love Languages.* Dr. Chapman argued that people give and receive love differently. He identified five ways to give and receive love—through words of affirmation, quality time, physical touch, gifts, or acts of service—and labeled these things as love languages. If you give love in a different language than a person receives it, then you can create frustration and separation in a relationship.

When it comes to loving God, His love language is obedience. When you follow His Word and spend time with Him in prayer and meditation, you show that you love Him. Loving God is essential to stewarding power well, because when you love Him, you submit your limited authority to Him and obey Him.

While loving God is essential to avoid the corruption of power, loving yourself is also important. I once heard a pastor say, "I have never met a man who beat his wife that liked himself."[15] When people don't like or love themselves, they are at constant war within, and whoever gets close to them gets the treatment they were already giving themselves.

When you don't love yourself, you won't know how to handle the people you have power over. You will abuse them because that's how you treat yourself. If you say negative things to yourself, you will say negative things to others. If you don't care about yourself, caring about others will be challenging. If you hate yourself, loving others will be hard.

Yet, when you love yourself, you see the world and situations through the eyes of love. You treat yourself well and speak to yourself with kindness. Your love for yourself will seep out in your actions, words, and empathy as you interact with others. And on the path to stewarding power well, loving others is the final step. Because when you don't love the people you have power over, you will abuse the power you hold.

Paul gave us the blueprint for love in 1 Corinthians: "Love is patient and kind. Love is not jealous or boastful or proud or rude. It does not demand its own way. It is not irritable, and it keeps no record of being wronged. It does not rejoice about injustice but rejoices whenever the truth wins out. Love never gives up, never loses faith, is always hopeful, and endures through every circumstance."[16] Paul's outline of love assumes offense as part of the process of love. For example, you will never be tempted to be irritable unless you are in a relationship with someone aggravating you. What Paul was getting at in his letter is that real love is on the other side of offense.

Many offenses can cause physical, emotional, systemic, and psychological harm. However, the most common offenses in everyday interpersonal relationships harm our pride more than anything. When we are hurt, our love is tested the most. The temptation for most of us is to love until it hurts and not when it hurts. But if we can love even when we are hurt, we are stewarding our God-given power well and breaking the corruption and trauma cycle.

The biblical character Joseph teaches us how to break the cycle of corruption and steward power well. After his father died, his brothers were concerned that Joseph would harm them because they had hurt him by selling him into slavery. They understood the power he had. Joseph was the second-in-command in all of Egypt. He could have had his brothers killed or imprisoned if he wanted to. However, instead of hurting them, Joseph kindly said, "Don't be afraid. Am I in the place of God? You intended to harm me, but God intended it for good to accomplish what is now being done, the saving of many lives. So then, don't be afraid. I will provide for you and your children."[17] Joseph countered their harm with love.

When you have control over others, especially those who have hurt you, how will you steward your power? Will you give Love control? If you do, fear will run, deception will fade, and your love for God and yourself will flow to others. The cycle of trauma and corruption will break, and your hurt soul will be able to turn to the source of healing: God.

THE HEALING POWER OF GOD

One Sunday morning, while in the second grade, I was sitting in the church balcony, enjoying service with my mother, when suddenly I began to have a seizure. My mother rushed me out, my father quickly left the front, and the usher called 911. That was my first time having a seizure, but it wasn't my last; I had another at home a few days later. My pediatrician scheduled a series of brain scans to help figure out the cause. Before my scan appointment, my parents took me to our church's prayer tower. Our bishop, the late Lawrence Callahan, and my parents joined their faith together and prayed fervently for me. When my scan reports came back, the doctor told my parents that my scans were completely normal and they couldn't find anything concerning. I never had a seizure again. God healed me.

While I'm thankful for the physical healing, I also know God is a healer of broken hearts. Over the years, I've watched Him repeatedly heal my heart when I've been hurt, betrayed, and abandoned by people I loved deeply. When Clark married someone else unexpectedly, God healed my heart. When I lost two best friends at once, God healed my heart and later restored the relationships. When my hero turned out not to be who I thought he was, God healed my heart. God is a heart healer.

Jesus wants you to bring your hurt to Him. He said, "Come to me, all of you who are weary and carry heavy burdens, and I will give you rest."[18] And the psalmist said, "The LORD is close to the brokenhearted; he rescues those whose spirits are crushed."[19]

Place your hope in the Healer, not in power.

I've experienced God's healing physically and emotionally, but the most extraordinary healing I received was of my sin-sick soul. Because of Adam's sin, I was born in sin and shaped in iniquity. There was nothing I could do to live right. Even the good I did wasn't good enough. However, one day I rec-

Place your hope in the Healer, not in power.

ognized that I was a sinner, cried out to God, repented, and accepted the finished work Jesus did through His death and resurrection. That was how God healed my soul. If you haven't experienced that healing, it's available to you.

You may be feeling physically or emotionally sick. Or you may feel the greatest sickness—a sin-sick soul. Friend, Jesus came for you, just like He came for me. He knew that "healthy people don't need a doctor—sick people do."[20] Your healing, like mine, comes through Jesus, not through the pursuit of power. He is the only one who can deliver on the healing He promises and the only one who can make you whole.

After trying everything—alternative spiritual practices, drugs, and alcohol—Daniel realized that nothing but God could truly make him whole. Daniel tried to take control after the accident, but he only ruined his life. He submitted to God's control, and God healed his sin-sick soul and restored his life.

In the synagogue, Jesus read Isaiah's prophecy about Himself from hundreds of years before:

The Spirit of the LORD is upon me,

    for he has anointed me to bring Good News to the

        poor.

He has sent me to proclaim that captives will be released,

    that the blind will see,

that the oppressed will be set free,

    and that the time of the LORD's favor has come.[21]

You see, only Jesus could bring the good news; only He could bring healing; only He had the power to save our sin-sick souls. Because only Jesus could afford the cost. Place your faith in Him.

PRAYER

God,

I have read this chapter, and I'm not sure how to feel. I understand where Lisa is coming from, but the pain is so intense and real. I want to avoid being hurt like that ever again. I don't know if I can trust Your power, because when I submitted my life to Your control in the past, I still experienced pain. So I took matters into my own hands, but honestly, my hands weren't able to stop the pain either.

I'm at a crossroads, and I'm not sure what to do.

Please help me trust that submitting to Your authority is best for me. Heal my heart, God; I want to be free from all this pain. Heal my mind and heal my soul. Help me steward the limited power You have given to me well.

In Jesus's name, amen.

CONCLUSION

PAIN REFRAMED

I know, somehow, that only when it is dark
enough can you see the stars.
—DR. MARTIN LUTHER KING, JR.,
"I've Been to the Mountaintop"

Throughout this book, I've tried to reframe the pain
you experience around personhood, peace, provision,
pleasure, purpose, protection, and power. While I know
what I shared doesn't alleviate the pain, I hope you now
have a renewed sense of faith and hope. Allow me to give
you one more piece of hope, one more ray of light, as you
wrestle in the gap between what you believe and what
you experience.

My relationship with a close friend ended abruptly. I
had moved to a new city and was still trying to adjust.
The responsibilities of traveling, speaking, and fundraising felt overwhelming. I was sharing my frustration and
heartbreak with my therapist, Dr. Stacy.

She leaned forward and gently said, "We often focus on the suffering Jesus experienced when we think of the pain that we are experiencing, but we miss that there is an actual resurrection."

I let her words wash over my bruised heart. There is a resurrection. The suffering doesn't last. My soul leaped. God doesn't leave us in the suffering. He gave us a way out. A place to turn to when life looks hopeless and bleak. He gave us hope.

In light of Jesus's resurrection, my suffering no longer looked hopeless and bleak. I had a way forward out of misery. A path toward healing because Jesus lives.

Friend, your pain is only a comma, not a period. You may be walking through the valley of the shadow of death, but you don't live there. God gives hope. Your hurt is a portal to new life, not just in the life to come but in this one so you can live it more abundantly.

Your pain is only a comma, not a period.

Let Peter's words be the balm you need to ease the pricks of pain: "The God of all grace, who called you to his eternal glory in Christ, after you have suffered a little while, will himself restore you and make you strong, firm and steadfast."[1]

As you spend time with the Lord, as you wrestle with Him and cry out, have faith that He will meet you in your pain. Have faith that He will heal you wherever it hurts. Remember, God loves you. He is for you. The Cross is proof. When your faith and trust are in Jesus, the suffering you experience in this world is only temporary. The Resurrection is proof. Jesus lives, and you will too.[2]

ACKNOWLEDGMENTS

Special thanks to the Jude 3 Project staff. I couldn't do what I do without you all. I'm blessed to work alongside you. I appreciate and love all of you.

NOTES

Chapter 1: Permission to Wrestle

1. Psalm 13:1–2, NIV.
2. Jeremiah 12:1.
3. Matthew 27:46.
4. Esau McCaulley, "Problematic Passages: What Should We Do When Bible Passages Bother Us? | Dr. Esau McCaulley," Jude 3 Project, YouTube, video, 11:45, June 16, 2021, www.youtube.com/watch?v=1MCztZNYDz8.
5. Bobby Barr, "Five Ways Businesses Can Use Amazon's Mission Statement as a Growth Strategy: The Customer-Centric Model of the World's Largest Retailer Is Perfect for Companies of Any Size," *Entrepreneur*, July 4, 2021, www.entrepreneur.com /growing-a-business/five-ways-businesses-can-use-amazons -mission-statement-as/373491.
6. Karen Weise and Michael Corkery, "People Now Spend More at Amazon Than at Walmart," *New York Times*, August 17, 2021, www.nytimes.com/2021/08/17/technology/amazon -walmart.html.
7. Matthew 4:23–25; Luke 9:10–17.
8. Psalm 16:11, ESV.
9. John 16:33, NIV.

Chapter 2: Personhood

1. Genesis 9:25.
2. Jemar Tisby, *The Color of Compromise: The Truth About the American Church's Complicity in Racism* (Grand Rapids, Mich.: Zondervan, 2019), 83.
3. U.S. Const., art. I, § 2, cl. 3.
4. Nicquel Terry Ellis, "A Black Family Says They 'Whitewashed' Their Home to Get a Higher Appraisal. They're Not the Only Ones," CNN, April 20, 2023, www.cnn.com/2023/04/15/us /real-estate-appraisals-bias-reaj/index.html.
5. Luke 4:18, ESV, emphasis added.
6. "Five Percent Nation: American Revisionist Movement," *Encyclopaedia Britannica,* updated January 27, 2024, www.britannica .com/topic/Five-Percent-Nation.
7. Genesis 1:27, NIV.
8. Genesis 3:5, NIV, emphasis added.
9. John Philip Jenkins, "White Supremacy," *Encyclopaedia Britannica,* updated March 21, 2024, www.britannica.com/topic /white-supremacy.
10. James 1:14–15, NIV.
11. Genesis 1:26, KJV.
12. "15 Amazing Attributes of God: What They Mean and Why They Matter," Bible Study Tools, updated February 15, 2024, www.biblestudytools.com/bible-study/topical-studies/15 -amazing-attributes-of-god-what-they-mean-and-why-they -matter.html.
13. Psalm 139:14, KJV.
14. Romans 8:38–39.
15. John 3:16.
16. Genesis 29–30.
17. 2 Corinthians 10:12, KJV.
18. Luke 4:1–13.

Chapter 3: Peace

1. Lizzie Duszynski-Goodman, "Mental Health Statistics and Facts," *Forbes,* February 21, 2024, www.forbes.com/health /mind/mental-health-statistics.

2. John 14:27, ᴇsᴠ.

3. Philippians 4:7.

4. Dharius Daniels, "Forgiveness," Jude 3 Project, Facebook video, December 23, 2016, www.facebook.com/jude3project/videos /1292878337399333.

5. Martin Luther King, Jr., *Stride Toward Freedom: The Montgomery Story* (Boston: Beacon, 2010), 27.

6. Philippians 4:6–7.

7. Isaiah 26:3.

Chapter 4: Provision

1. Philippians 4:19.

2. Psalm 73:2–5.

3. 1 Kings 17:7–16.

4. Matthew 6:31–33.

5. Matthew 7:9–11.

6. Umar Johnson, "Dr Umar Johnson Black Church 'Ground Zero' Documentary," John Rodgers, video, 1:41, January 27, 2015, https://youtu.be/8B7gUTvLXeg.

7. Yana Conner and Lisa Fields, *Through Eyes of Color: A Contextualized Guide to Help You Know What You Believe and Why* (Jacksonville, Fla.: Jude 3 Project, 2019), 40–41.

8. Deuteronomy 24:14.

9. Proverbs 22:22–23.

10. Proverbs 29:7.

11. Jeremiah 5:27–28, ɴɪᴠ.

12. Amos 5:24.

13. James 1:27.

14. James 1:2–4.

15. Luke 5:1–11.

16. Numbers 11:4–6.

17. Mother Teresa, "Mother Teresa: Acceptance Speech" (speech, University of Oslo, Oslo, Norway, December 10, 1979), www.nobelprize.org/prizes/peace/1979/teresa/acceptance -speech.

18. 2 Corinthians 9:10–11, ᴄᴇᴠ.

19. Matthew 25:42–45, ɴɪᴠ.

20. Matthew 25:41, NIV.
21. Luke 12:48.
22. *Merriam-Webster,* s.v. "gentrification," accessed January 25, 2024, www.merriam-webster.com/dictionary/gentrification.
23. Luke 19:8, NIV.

Chapter 5: Pleasure

1. Ecclesiastes 2:10–11.
2. Jim Carrey, "Jim Carrey at MIU: Commencement Address at the 2014 Graduation" (speech, Maharishi International University, Fairfield, Iowa, May 24, 2014), www.youtube.com/watch?v=V80-gPkpH6M.
3. Genesis 2:16–17.
4. Paul Tripp, "The Doctrine of Holiness," Paul Tripp, September 10, 2018, www.paultripp.com/articles/posts/the-doctrine-of-holiness-article.
5. Isaiah 6:3, ESV.
6. Da' T.R.U.T.H., "Click (No Regrets)," track 15 on *Open Book,* Cross Movement Records, 2007.
7. G. K. Chesterton, *The Thing: Why I Am a Catholic* (New York: Dodd, Mead, 1930), 27.
8. John 10:10.
9. Proverbs 10:22, KJV.
10. John 10:10, NKJV.
11. Matthew 6:19–20.
12. Revelation 21:4.

Chapter 6: Purpose

1. Romans 8:28, KJV.
2. 2 Timothy 2:3.
3. Martin Luther King, Jr., "I've Been to the Mountaintop" (speech, Mason Temple, Memphis, Tenn., April 3, 1968), https://kinginstitute.stanford.edu/ive-been-mountaintop.
4. 2 Corinthians 12:9, NIV.
5. Hebrews 12:15, ESV.
6. Matthew 5:23–24.
7. Matthew 18:15.

Chapter 7: Protection

1. Vince Vitale, "Why Series | Why Suffering: Suffering and the Love of God | Vince Vitale," RZIM HQ, video, 43:10, July 1, 2016, https://youtu.be/v2fWxoqiXco.
2. Ephesians 1:11, NKJV.
3. Job 38:4–13.
4. Timothy Keller (@timkellernyc), X, August 13, 2022, https://twitter.com/timkellernyc/status/1558475971073818626?lang=en.
5. Genesis 1:26, ESV.
6. Dharius Daniels, "The Breaking Point // Damaged but Not Destroyed (Part 8) // Dr. Dharius Daniels," Transformation Church, video, 59:17, November 19, 2023, https://youtu.be/dzAUkYhjSBE?feature=shared.
7. The Notorious B.I.G., "Mo Money Mo Problems," featuring Mase and Puff Daddy, track 10 on *Life After Death,* Bad Boy Records, 1997.
8. Job 2:10, NKJV.
9. Genesis 50:20, NIV.
10. John 11:21, 32.
11. Romans 8:28, NIV.
12. Matthew 27:46, NIV.

Chapter 8: Power

1. Emily Rekstis, "Healing Crystals 101: Everything You Need to Know," Healthline, updated November 14, 2023, www.healthline.com/health/mental-health/guide-to-healing-crystals.
2. Adrian White, "10 Benefits of Burning Sage, How to Get Started, and More," Healthline, updated February 3, 2023, www.healthline.com/health/benefits-of-burning-sage.
3. Proverbs 16:9.
4. The Carters, "Boss," track 3 on *Everything Is Love,* Roc Nation, 2018.
5. Matthew 28:18.
6. Jeremiah 10:23.
7. Acts 1:8.
8. "Joe Biden Loses First Wife and Daughter in Tragic Car Acci-

dent," History.com, June 2, 2023, www.history.com/this-day
-in-history/joe-biden-loses-first-wife-and-daughter-in-tragic
-car-accident.

9. Meredith Newman, "What Joe Biden Learned from His Life-
Threatening Brain Aneurysms," Delaware Online, March 18,
2019, www.delawareonline.com/story/news/politics/joe
-biden/2019/03/18/joe-biden-2020-how-then-senator
-overcame-life-threatening-brain-aneurysms/3002961002.

10. Randall Chase, "Vice President's Son Beau Biden Dies at 46 of
Brain Cancer," Associated Press, May 31, 2015, https://apnews
.com/general-news-d8f69eb645d74b7886387f713981b739.

11. Philip Elliott, "Hunter Biden on Making His Own Crack, Living with His Dealer and His Family's Effort to Keep Him
Alive," *Time,* April 6, 2021, https://time.com/5952773
/hunter-biden-memoir-beautiful-things.

12. 1 John 4:18, kjv.

13. Becky Little, "Why Bibles Given to Slaves Omitted Most of
the Old Testament," History.com, updated August 24, 2023,
www.history.com/news/slave-bible-redacted-old-testament.

14. Anthony Schmidt, quoted in Michel Martin, "Slave Bible
from the 1800s Omitted Key Passages That Could Incite Re-
bellion," NPR, December 9, 2018, www.npr.org/2018/12/09
/674995075/slave-bible-from-the-1800s-omitted-key-passages
-that-could-incite-rebellion.

15. T. D. Jakes, "TD Jakes Sermons: Love Has No Loopholes
Part 1," video, 28:30, March 22, 2013, https://youtu.be/o2AW
jk3tClE?feature=shared.

16. 1 Corinthians 13:4–7.

17. Genesis 50:19–21, niv.

18. Matthew 11:28.

19. Psalm 34:18.

20. Luke 5:31.

21. Luke 4:18–19.

Conclusion: Pain Reframed

1. 1 Peter 5:10, niv.

2. John 14:19.

Lisa Victoria Fields, one of the world's most sought-after Christian apologists, combines her passion for biblical literacy with her heart for sharing God's love with all those she meets. She is the founder and CEO of Jude 3 Project. Lisa has received several honors, including being recognized in *Christianity Today* for her work as an apologist in the African American community. She helped produce two documentaries—*Unspoken,* an in-depth look into the Christian heritage of Africa and people of African descent, and *Juneteenth: Faith and Freedom*—through her partnership with Our Daily Bread. Lisa earned a bachelor of science in communications and religious studies from the University of North Florida and a master of divinity with a focus in theology from Liberty University.

KNOW WHAT YOU BELIEVE.
KNOW WHY YOU BELIEVE.

JUDE 3 PROJECT

Founded by apologist and author Lisa Victoria Fields, Jude 3 Project is a ministry organization dedicated to helping Black Christians know what they believe and why they believe it. Jude 3 Project achieves its mission through transformative events, curriculum, online courses, thoughtfully curated discussions, and engaging storytelling through film and multimedia.

Learn more at jude3project.org